moorish

moorish

GREG AND LUCY MALOUF

APPLE

First published in the UK in 2006
by Apple Press
Sheridan House
114 Western Road
Hove
East Sussex BN3 1DD
www.apple-press.com

First published in Australia in 2001
by Hardie Grant Books
85 High Street
Prahran
Victoria 3181
Australia
www.hardiegrant.com.au

ISBN 1 84543 115 4

978 1 84543 115 0

Cover and text design by
Klarissa Pfisterer and Hamish Freeman
Photography by Matt Harvey
Typeset by J & M Typesetting
Produced by SNP Leefung Printers Ltd
Printed and bound in China

acknowledgements

From beginning to end, this book has
been a joy to write, and the process
made even more pleasurable by the help
we have received from numerous people
along the way.

Our particular thanks go to Kurt Sampson
and Adrian Smith, for cooking the dishes
that were photographed for the book.
Our gratitude also, to Con and George at
Clamms Seafood, Roger, Simon and Sylvio
at Lago's Butchers, Geoff, Amal and Dodo
from Café Zum Zum and all the wonderful
people at Greengrocer.com for providing
such terrific ingredients.

Thanks also, to Sandy Grant for asking
us to write a second book, and to everyone
at Hardie Grant who worked so tirelessly
on it. Our particular appreciation goes
to Julie Pinkham and Mary Small, and
to Foong Ling Kong for her patient and
skilful editing. Our deepest and most
heartfelt thanks go to Tracy O'Shaughnessy
for her encouragement, commitment and
friendship. Thank you, too, to Matt Harvey
for his beautiful photographs, and to
designers Klarissa Pfisterer and Hamish
Freeman who have made the book look
so gorgeous.

Finally, thank you to our parents,
in particular our mothers, who instilled
in us a love of good food and culinary
adventure from our earliest years.

CONTENTS

introduction

We are shameless! We want to seduce you: to stimulate your imagination, invigorate your senses and tempt you to try the wonderful flavours and dishes of Moorish food.

By Moorish, what we mean, loosely, is the cuisine that sprang up as a result of the Arabic occupation of North Africa in the eighth century. Over the centuries, though, Moorish food has absorbed not just the exotic range of spices, herbs, fruit and vegetables introduced by the Arabs, but also the later influences of the Ottoman Empire and new and different ingredients from the New World.

One of the most exciting things about this style of cooking is that for most of us, it is still relatively new and unexplored. Sure, we all know about tabbouleh and take-away felafel, and harissa and couscous have become de rigueur on trendy bistro menus in recent years, but most of us still don't know and understand Moorish food in the same way that we know and understand English, Italian and French food or the more recently fashionable dishes of Asia.

Largely, this is due to a lack of resources – after all, there are thousands of books on how to cook Italian food or Chinese food, but relatively few about food from the Middle East and North Africa or even the Eastern Mediterranean. And those dishes that we are familiar with tend to belong to a limited range of strictly traditional fare.

But our clear and undisguised mission in life is for people to become as comfortable with the ingredients, techniques and dishes of Moorish food as they already are with those from the Mediterranean. We want you to be able to whip up chermoula as readily as pesto; to be as comfortable with tagines as with casseroles. We want spices such as sumac and saffron to become as much a part of your repertoire as basil and rosemary.

Thankfully, this is not about transforming your kitchen into a spice bazaar – while some of the spices and ingredients might be new to you, and may require a trip to a deli or Middle Eastern grocer, most of the ingredients you need for the recipes that follow, you'll already have on hand. What we hope to try and teach you, though, is how to use them in the best Moorish tradition, if not necessarily in traditional dishes. We want you to learn how to use what might even already be familiar ingredients in new and exciting ways to transform the mundane into something exotic.

In our view, the point of difference in all good cooking comes when you can be inventive and creative; when you are comfortable enough with ingredients and dishes to throw recipes and precise measurements to the wind and start to have fun in the kitchen. When you begin to rely on your tastebuds and instinct rather than slavishly following written instructions. And this is how all great cooks (and chefs) practise their art – with handfuls and scoops rather than grams and millilitres.

This is no more true than in the kitchen at home. We all know the relief of being able to knock up an old favourite - be it scrambled eggs, or spaghetti Bolognese or a Victoria sponge for tea. There is something wonderfully liberating about working on auto-pilot in the kitchen – about having dishes in one's repertoire that almost make themselves.

It comes with practise, of course, and there's the rub. How can you be that comfortable with a cuisine that is relatively new and unfamiliar? When you don't know what things are meant to taste like? How much easier is it to stick to the old favourites? But stop for a minute and think back to the days (not so very long ago, after all) when few of us recognised the taste of lemongrass or even basil or chilli. To understand new ingredients and flavour combinations, all that is really required is a sense of adventure.

This book begins, therefore, with a section on the spice mixes, dressings, relishes, pickles and preserves that best define Moorish cooking – and with these recipes we suggest that you do follow the quantities carefully, so that you become familiar with the intended flavours and textures. But from here on in, let your imagination run wild! Follow our suggestions, and use baharat, for instance, to transform a humble roast lamb; or tabil to spice up a warming lentil soup; fry chicken schnitzel in cumin butter for a change; or braise oxtail with cinnamon and preserved lemon; make tiramisu a little different by using Turkish coffee instead of espresso, and flavour a simple junket with rosewater to make it truly exotic.

You will soon find that you are limited only by your own imagination, and that you will be using Moorish flavours with abandon in your own day to day cooking! Before you know it, you too will be able to transform the most mundane ingredients lurking in your fridge into a delicious and imaginative Moorish meal.

DRY SPICE MIXES

Baharat

5 tablespoons sweet paprika

4 tablespoons black pepper, finely ground

3 tablespoons cumin seeds, finely ground

2 tablespoons coriander seeds, finely ground

2 tablespoons cinnamon powder

2 tablespoons cloves, finely ground

1 tablespoon cardamom seeds, finely ground

1 tablespoon ground star anise

1 teaspoon grated nutmeg

Baharat means, literally, 'spices', and Arab households purchase this all-purpose mix by the sack-load from specialist spice shops. As with many spice blends, there are variations on the basic theme, and recipes vary according to region and family. The overall flavour of baharat is similar to allspice, and it is used extensively in marinades, braises and stews.

Simply mix all the ingredients in a jar with a tight-fitting lid, and shake to combine well. It will keep for up to a year.
Makes about 200 g (7 oz)

WE USE BAHARAT FOR:
Roast Leg of Lamb with Baharat
Root Vegetables (page 104)
Rockling Braised with Arabic Spices
and Angel Hair Pasta (page 130)

Coriander Salt

4 tablespoons coriander seeds

2 teaspoons cumin seeds

3 tablespoons sea salt

Little bowls of spiced salts are wonderful to have on the table for dipping, or sprinkling on food as it is eaten. Spiced salt can be rubbed onto meat before grilling, or into the skin of poultry before it is fried. Reverse the quantities of coriander and cumin to make cumin salt, which is equally delicious.

Lightly roast, grind and sieve the coriander and cumin seeds. Grind the salt to a fine powder.
   Heat a non-stick frying pan and warm the salt, coriander and cumin powders together so they merge into one fragrant powder. Store in an airtight jar for up to 6 months.
Makes 60 g (2 oz)

WE USE CORIANDER SALT FOR:
Crisp Egyptian Pigeon with Coriander Salt (page 98)

Ras al Hanout

1 teaspoon cumin seeds
1 teaspoon coriander seeds
6 cardamom pods, seeds only
$^1/_2$ teaspoon fennel seeds
$^1/_2$ teaspoon black peppercorns
2 teaspoons sweet paprika
1 teaspoon cinnamon powder
1 teaspoon turmeric
1 teaspoon cayenne pepper
1 teaspoon salt
$^1/_2$ teaspoon sugar
$^1/_2$ teaspoon allspice

A secret blend of herbs and spices from Morocco. Every spice vendor has his own ras al hanout blends, which vary in price according to the scarcity of the ingredients. The most prized and exotic blends can include thirty or more spices, plant roots and other unusual aromatics. For daily use, cooks tend to use a humbler blend similar to the one below. Use ras al hanout in soups and tagines, with rice and couscous, or mix it with a little oil and rub onto meat or poultry as a marinade.

Lightly roast and finely grind the cumin, coriander, cardamom, fennel and peppercorns, then sieve to remove the husks. Mix with the rest of the ingredients and store in an airtight jar. The mixture keeps well for up to 3 months.
Makes 50 g (1$^1/_2$ oz)

WE USE RAS AL HANOUT FOR:
Prawn Fattouche with Turkish Bread (page 47)
Giant Couscous (page 81)
Quail with Limes and Ras al Hanout (page 96)
Shish Kifte (page 108)
Ceviche of Red Mullet with Ras al Hanout (page 129)
Fricasseed Prawns with Leeks and Saffron (page 134)

Za'atar

1/3 cup sumac

1 cup za'atar

100 ml (3 1/2 fl oz) olive oil

Za'atar is the Arabic word for wild thyme, and for the spice mix made with the herb, roasted sesame seeds and the ground sour red berries of the sumac tree. It is dearly beloved in the Middle East, where it is eaten virtually daily, sprinkled on dishes as a garnish, or mixed with olive oil to make a paste. Greg always has a little jar of it in the fridge, which he eats on toast for breakfast instead of Vegemite!

To make za'atar, you need to buy a bag of ground sumac and a bag of za'atar (which will actually be a mixture of wild thyme and sesame seeds) from a Middle Eastern food store. Combine the two in a ratio of three za'atar to one sumac (it makes sense to begin with a tablespoon measure) and store in an airtight jar.

Alternatively, stir in enough olive oil to make a loose paste. Store in a sealed jar in the fridge, where it will keep quite happily for a couple of months.

Makes 130 g (4 1/3 oz)

WE USE ZA'ATAR FOR:
Lamb's Brains with Za'atar Crumbs, Bacon and Apple Butter (page 118)

Dukkah

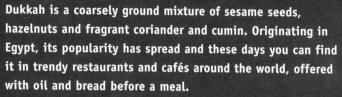

50 g (1½ oz) hazelnuts
8 tablespoons sesame seeds
4 tablespoons coriander seeds
3 tablespoons cumin seeds
1 teaspoon sea salt
½ teaspoon freshly ground black pepper

Dukkah is a coarsely ground mixture of sesame seeds, hazelnuts and fragrant coriander and cumin. Originating in Egypt, its popularity has spread and these days you can find it in trendy restaurants and cafés around the world, offered with oil and bread before a meal.

Don't feel constrained to use it only as a dip – it is terrific sprinkled on all kinds of salads, and works particularly well with the unctuous richness of soft-boiled eggs.

Roast the hazelnuts, sesame seeds, coriander and cumin seeds separately in a hot, dry frying pan. Keep an eye on the heat – it should not be so hot that the seeds and nuts burn or colour too quickly. Shake the pan gently from time to time so that they brown evenly, then tip straightaway onto kitchen paper.

With the roasted hazelnuts, tip them into a tea-towel and rub them briskly between your fingers to loosen and flake away the dark papery skin.

To grind the ingredients, you may use the traditional mortar and pestle, or a speedier food processor, or spice (coffee) grinder. You can grind the coriander and cumin seeds together, but do the sesame seeds and hazelnuts separately – be careful not to overgrind or you run the risk of ending up with an oily paste, rather than the desired coarsely ground crumb.

Mix the nuts and seeds with the salt and pepper and store the dukkah in an airtight jar in the refrigerator, where it will keep for several weeks.
Makes 200 g (7 oz)

WE USE DUKKAH FOR:
Black Pudding with Egyptian Fried Egg (page 116)

WET SPICE MIXES

Chermoula

2 tablespoons cumin seeds, lightly roasted and finely ground

1 tablespoon coriander seeds, lightly roasted and finely ground

1¹/₂ tablespoons sweet paprika

1 tablespoon ground ginger

2 cloves garlic, roughly chopped

2–4 whole bullet chillies, seeded, scraped and roughly chopped

juice of 2 lemons

100 ml (3¹/₂ fl oz) olive oil

¹/₂ teaspoon sea salt

¹/₂ teaspoon freshly ground black pepper

Chermoula is one of the signature spices of North Africa. It is most often used as a fragrant marinade for seafood dishes, but also works well with poultry and meat. The dominant flavours are garlic, cumin, paprika, coriander and lemon, and a chilli content that varies according to your taste.

Put all the ingredients into a food processor and blitz until the garlic and chillies are ground to a paste. Tip into a clean jar and cover with olive oil. It will keep in the refrigerator for up to 6 months. Top up with a little oil each time you use it.

For *Tomato Chermoula* add 250 g (8 oz) crushed tomatoes

For *Green Onion Chermoula* add 100 g (3¹/₂ oz) finely minced spring onions (scallions).

Makes 200 g (7 oz)

WE USE CHERMOULA FOR:
French Lentils Sautéed with Bulgarian Fetta (page 86)
Baby Octopus Chargrilled with Moroccan Spices (page 125)
Eggplant and Fetta Stir-fry (page 141)

Tabil

1½ cups fresh coriander
(cilantro), roots removed

1 tablespoon caraway seeds,
roasted and crushed

½ head garlic, cloves peeled

1 red pepper, roasted and peeled

6 bullet chillies, seeded,
scraped and finely chopped

80 ml (2¾ fl oz) olive oil

A very hot salsa from North Africa.

Place all the ingredients, except the olive oil, in a food
processor and whiz together. Slowly add the oil to make
a smooth paste. Tip into a jar, seal with a thin layer
of olive oil and refrigerate. This
will keep for around a week.
Makes 300 ml (10 fl oz)

WE USE TABIL FOR:
Devilled Green Lentil Soup
with Candied Ham Hock
(page 34)

Taklia

6 cloves garlic, sliced

1 tablespoon olive oil

2 teaspoons ground coriander

1 teaspoon sea salt

Taklia is another very simple, all-purpose savoury mix
found in Lebanon and Syria. It is usually added at the end
of cooking for its aromatic flavouring. It can also be thinned
down with a little olive oil and used as a condiment,
or enlivened with a touch of chilli.

Place the garlic and olive oil in a heavy-based pan and sauté
for 1 minute, taking care not to let it colour. Put the garlic
into a mortar with the coriander and salt and grind to a very
thick paste. Spoon into a jar. It will keep for up to 2 months
in the fridge.
Makes 40 g (1¼ oz)

WE USE TAKLIA FOR:
Buttered Egg Noodles with Artichokes, Cèpes and Saffron
(page 82)
Chicken Roasted with Forty Cloves of Garlic and Merguez
Sausages (page 91)
Lamb Baked with Orzo Pasta, Tomatoes and Lemon (page 105)

DRESSINGS & RELISHES

Tahini–Yoghurt Sauce

180 ml (6 fl oz) plain yoghurt
60 ml (2 fl oz) tahini paste
juice of up to 1 lemon
1 clove garlic, crushed with
1 teaspoon sea salt

Tahini is probably best known for the part it plays in
providing a nutty base note to dips such as hummus and baba
ghanoush. It is enormously popular around the Middle East,
where it is also used, thinned down with water and flavoured
with garlic and lemon juice, as a sauce for cold baked fish.
On its own, it can be too strong and bitter for European
palates, but combined with yoghurt, it becomes smooth
and creamy with a mysteriously earthy flavour.

Combine the yoghurt, tahini, lemon juice and garlic paste.
Thin with a little water if necessary – the sauce should have
the consistency of thin honey. Taste and adjust the flavours as
necessary. What you are aiming for is a good balance of sharp
yoghurt and lemon with garlic and nutty tahini. Refrigerate
and use within 2–3 days.
Makes 250 ml (8 fl oz)

SERVE TAHINI–YOGHURT SAUCE WITH:
Eggplant Salad with Tahini–Yoghurt Dressing (page 42)
Haloumi Baked in Vine Leaves (page 52)
Cheese-stuffed Kataifi (page 56)
Roast Quail Stuffed with Rice and Nuts (page 97)
Duck Shish Kebab (page 102)
Lamb Kibbeh Stuffed with Mozzarella and Pine Nuts
(page 106)
Shish Kifte (page 108)
Grilled Snapper with Tahini–Yoghurt Dressing (page 132)

Toum

1 whole head garlic

1 teaspoon sea salt

juice of 1 lemon

200 ml (7 fl oz) sunflower oil

2 tablespoons water

Strictly for garlic lovers, there is no compromise with this intense sauce. Uncooked, garlic has a uniquely hot pungency. But when combined with an emulsion of oil and lemon juice, it softens to become smooth and almost fluffy. There is simply nothing like it for serving with grilled chicken.

Peel and roughly chop the garlic cloves, then put them into a blender or liquidiser with the salt and lemon juice. Blend until very smooth, which will take around 2 minutes. Scrape down the sides from time to time to make sure no chunks of garlic get left out of the paste.

Next, very slowly start to add the oil. You need to imagine you are making a mayonnaise, so start slowly, emulsifying each addition well before adding more oil. Continue to dribble in the oil until it is fully absorbed. Finally, add the water. The whole process should take no longer than about 5 minutes.

If the sauce splits as you're making it, you can save it by doing the following. Clean out the liquidiser. Put in 2 egg yolks and blend, then, very slowly pour in half the split mixture. When it begins to emulsify and thicken, add a teaspoon of cold water to loosen it. Then gradually add the rest of the mix. You end up with a straight mayonnaise rather than a sauce, but it is equally delicious!

The sauce keeps refrigerated for about a week.

Makes 300 ml (10 fl oz)

SERVE TOUM WITH:

Chicken Baked with Almond Crumbs (page 88)

Maple-roasted Quail (page 93)

Crisp Egyptian Pigeon with Coriander Salt (page 98)

Chilli-charred Squab (page 100)

Duck Shish Kebab (page 102)

Shish Kifte (page 108)

Veal Cutlets with Pine Nuts, Rosemary and Orange Crumbs (page 112)

Cumin-fried Whitebait (page 127)

Walnut–Pomegranate Dressing

150 g (5 oz) walnuts, roasted and the skins rubbed off

1 cup coriander (cilantro) leaves, finely shredded

1 small purple onion, finely diced

1 mild long red chilli, seeded, scraped and roughly chopped

juice of 1 lemon

80 ml (2½ fl oz) extra virgin olive oil

1 teaspoon pomegranate molasses

A variation on the traditional nut sauce known as tarator, which is frequently served with fish around the Middle East both hot and cold. We particularly like it with firm-fleshed white fish such as snapper. The slight sharpness of the pomegranate molasses also makes it exceptionally good with oily fish such as salmon. Try it in cold vegetable salads, or drizzle a little over green beans or zucchini. Make this dressing at the last minute to keep the coriander leaves green and fresh.

Put the walnuts, coriander, onion and chilli into a mixing bowl. Add the lemon juice, oil and pomegranate molasses and mix everything together well.

Makes around 150 ml (5 fl oz), enough for 4 servings

SERVE WALNUT–POMEGRANATE DRESSING WITH:
Chilli-charred Squab (page 100)
Shish Kifte (page 108)
Oysters with Lebanese Sausages (page 120)
Cumin-fried Whitebait (page 127)
Grilled Snapper with Walnut–Pomegranate
Dressing (page 133)
Mushroom Brochettes with Molten Haloumi (page 145)

Juniper Berry Dressing with Preserved Lemons

2 egg yolks

1 teaspoon Dijon mustard

1 tablespoon sherry vinegar

juice of $^1/_2$ lemon

$^1/_2$ tablespoon freshly ground black pepper

1 tablespoon juniper berries, crushed

300 ml (10 fl oz) olive oil

120 ml (4 fl oz) water

1 tablespoon diced Preserved Lemons (see pages 20–1) peel

One of our favourite dressings.

In a blender at medium speed combine the egg yolks, mustard, vinegar, lemon juice, pepper and juniper berries. Slowly add the oil until the dressing thickens.
   Add half the water, then the remaining oil, followed by the rest of the water. The dressing should have a honey-like consistency. Pour into a bowl and add the preserved lemon. Check the seasoning and add salt if necessary. Makes 500 ml (1 pint)

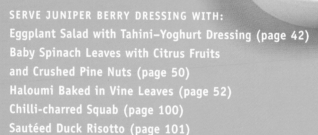

SERVE JUNIPER BERRY DRESSING WITH:
Eggplant Salad with Tahini–Yoghurt Dressing (page 42)
Baby Spinach Leaves with Citrus Fruits and Crushed Pine Nuts (page 50)
Haloumi Baked in Vine Leaves (page 52)
Chilli-charred Squab (page 100)
Sautéed Duck Risotto (page 101)

Green Harissa

125 g (4 oz) large green chillies, seeded, scraped and shredded

1 clove garlic

100 g (3$^1/_2$ oz) fresh spinach leaves, stalks removed

2 cups fresh coriander (cilantro) leaves, roots removed

1 teaspoon caraway seeds, roasted and crushed

1 teaspoon coriander seeds, roasted and crushed

1 teaspoon dried mint

$^1/_2$ teaspoon chilli powder

60 ml (2 fl oz) olive oil

An adaptation of the more commonly found red harissa, green harissa is more fragrant than fiery, with a milder and sweeter taste. The coriander makes it more refreshing.

Place all the ingredients except for the oil in a food processor. Whiz for a minute, and then, with the machine still running, slowly add the oil until the mixture is the consistency of pouring cream. Season with salt and pepper. Pour into a jar, top with a thin layer of olive oil and refrigerate. It will keep for around a week. Makes 250 ml (8 fl oz)

WE USE GREEN HARISSA FOR:
Salmon and Mint Briouats (page 55)
Mussels, Leeks and Pernod with Taramasalata Toasts (page 124)

Red Harissa

1 red pepper, whole

10–15 dried red chillies

10 small bullet chillies

2 cloves garlic

1/2 teaspoon sea salt

1 teaspoon cumin seeds, roasted and crushed

3/4 teaspoon caraway seeds, roasted and crushed

60 ml (2 fl oz) olive oil

At its simplest, harissa is rehydrated dried chillies mixed with tomato paste and salt. You'll find it on every table in Morocco as a chilli sauce, which tends to get drizzled on everything.

This version is the one we used in Arabesque; it is slightly more complex than the simplest Moroccan versions. It might seem like an unbelievably large number of chillies, and yes, do approach with caution!

Preheat the oven to 200°C (400°F).

Place the pepper on a baking tray and roast until the skin starts to blister and blacken, turning from time to time. Remove from the oven and tip into a bowl. Cover with cling film and leave to steam for a further 10 minutes, which softens the pepper and loosens the skin. Carefully peel away the skin and discard the stalk and seeds.

Pour enough boiling water over the dried chillies and leave them to rehydrate for about 10 minutes. Seed the bullet chillies, but leave the white inner fibres intact. Crush the garlic with the salt.

Place all the ingredients in a blender and purée with the olive oil. Taste carefully for seasoning – it is extremely hot – adding more salt if necessary. Tip into a jar and pour on a thin layer of olive oil. It will keep for 3–4 weeks in the refrigerator.

Makes about 200 ml (7 fl oz)

WE USE RED HARISSA FOR:

Potato and Mussel Salad with Harissa Dressing (page 41)

Fried Parmesan Polenta with Tomato Harissa (page 77)

Lemon Chicken Fricassee with Honey-cured Bacon (page 92)

Hilbeh

2 tablespoons fenugreek seeds,
lightly pounded to crack them

125 ml (4 fl oz) water

4 cloves garlic

1 cup chopped coriander
(cilantro) leaves

1/2–1 teaspoon sea salt

juice of 1 lemon

2 small hot green chillies

Hilbeh is an unusual fenugreek relish, with a spicy, almost
curry-like flavour. It needs to be made a day ahead, as the
fenugreek seeds have to be soaked to reduce their bitterness,
and to release their strange jelly-like texture.

Soak the fenugreek seeds in cold water overnight until a slight
gelatinous coating appears on the seeds and the soaking liquid
begins to froth. Drain off the water.

Put the fenugreek in a food processor with the garlic and
coriander leaves and whiz to a coarse paste. Add the salt,
lemon juice and chillies and enough cold water just to cover
the blades of the processor and process again. Tip into
a sealed jar and refrigerate. It will keep for a week.
Makes 150 ml (5 fl oz)

WE USE HILBEH FOR:
Tunisian Lamb Soup with Almonds and Fenugreek (page 35)
Eggplant Rice Pilaf with Hilbeh and Yoghurt (page 71)

Zhoug

4 cardamom pods

1 teaspoon black peppercorns

1 teaspoon caraway seeds

2 cups fresh coriander
(cilantro), roots removed

4–6 bullet chillies,
seeded and scraped

6 cloves garlic

1/4 teaspoon sea salt

a splash of water

A fiery-hot chilli relish that comes originally from Yemen
but has now become a firm favourite in Israel. Like hilbeh,
it is eaten with bread as an accompaniment to just about
everything, and works particularly well with fish, meats and
chicken dishes. Its ferocious chilli heat makes it addictive!

Crush the cardamom pods, peppercorns and caraway seeds
in a mortar and pestle, then sift to remove the husks.

Wash and thoroughly dry the coriander. Put the chillies,
coriander, garlic, salt and water in a blender, add the spices
and mix well. Tip into a jar and seal with 1 tablespoon
olive oil. It will keep for around a week in the refrigerator.
Makes 100 ml (3 1/2 fl oz)

WE USE ZHOUG FOR:
Couscous Stew with Grilled
Calamari and Zhoug (page 79)

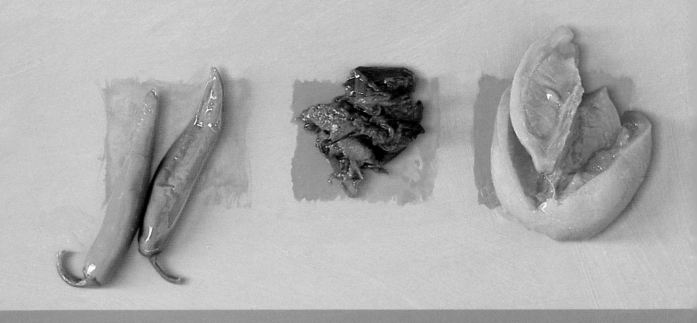

PICKLES & PRESERVES

Preserved Lemons and Limes

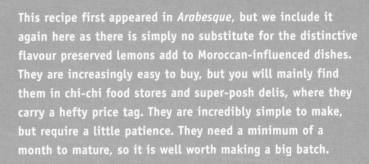

1.5 kg (3 lb) thin-skinned
lemons or limes

350 g (11½ oz) sea salt

1 tablespoon coriander
seeds, lightly crushed

2 cinnamon sticks

2 lemon leaves or bay leaves

2 tablespoons honey

250 ml (8 fl oz) lemon juice

750 ml (24 fl oz) warm water

This recipe first appeared in *Arabesque*, but we include it again here as there is simply no substitute for the distinctive flavour preserved lemons add to Moroccan-influenced dishes. They are increasingly easy to buy, but you will mainly find them in chi-chi food stores and super-posh delis, where they carry a hefty price tag. They are incredibly simple to make, but require a little patience. They need a minimum of a month to mature, so it is well worth making a big batch.

Wash and dry the lemons. Cut them lengthways into quarters, from the point of the lemon to three-quarters of the way down, but leave them joined together at the base. Place them in a plastic bag in the freezer for 24 hours. This dramatically speeds up the maturing process.

Defrost the lemons. Stuff the centre of each lemon with a heaped teaspoon of salt. Arrange them neatly in a 2 litre jar, sprinkling each layer with more salt and crushed coriander seeds as you go. Stuff the cinnamon sticks into the jar with the lemon leaves.

Mix the honey and lemon juice with the warm water until the honey dissolves. Pour into the jar so that the lemons are completely covered. Screw on the lid and put the jar into a large pot on top of a piece of cardboard (this stops the jar vibrating). Pour in enough warm water to come halfway up the sides of the jar and slowly bring it to the boil. Boil for 6 minutes, then remove from the heat. Lift the jar out of the water and store in a cool, dry place for at least a month before opening. Once opened, keep refrigerated.

Makes 1.5 kg (3 lb)

WE USE PRESERVED LEMONS FOR:
Chicken Soup with Egg and Lemon and
Bird's Nest Pasta (page 26)
Preserved Lemon Risotto (page 70)
Buttered Egg Noodles with Artichokes, Cèpes
and Saffron (page 82)
Chicken Schnitzel Fried in Cumin Butter (page 89)
Lemon Chicken Fricassee with Honey-cured Bacon (page 92)
Lamb Baked with Orzo Pasta, Tomatoes and Lemon
(page 105)
Oxtail Braised with Cinnamon and Preserved Lemon
(page 109)
Sautéed Fennel and Tomato Couscous (page 139)

Green Coconut Chutney

4 cups coriander (cilantro),
stalks and roots

2 cups mint leaves

6 cloves garlic

2 teaspoons ground cumin

1 teaspoon ground white pepper

1 teaspoon sugar

1 teaspoon sea salt

75 ml (2¹/₂ fl oz) lime juice

8 long green chillies

100 ml (3¹/₂ fl oz) coconut cream

100 ml (3¹/₂ fl oz) thickened
cream (or yoghurt)

2¹/₂ tablespoons honey

3 slices white bread, crusts
removed and diced

This is a wonderfully refreshing chutney, delicious eaten as
an accompaniment to hot spicy braises and tagines. We like
it so much that we eat it with just about everything from
grilled meat and chicken to soups and Indian curries –
and sometimes just on its own with warm pitta bread.
The quantities might seem quite large, but you'll find
that it disappears very quickly.

Place all the ingredients in a food processor and blend at
high speed until smooth. Check for seasoning – it may need
more salt and pepper. Spoon into a clean jar, cover with a
film of vegetable oil and refrigerate if not using immediately.
It will keep for up to 10 days.
Makes 500 ml (16 fl oz)

SERVE GREEN COCONUT CHUTNEY WITH:
Greek Leek Croquettes (page 53)
Salmon and Mint Briouats (page 55)
Cheese-stuffed Kataifi (page 56)
Chicken Tagine with Green Herb Couscous (page 94)
Chilli-charred Squab (page 100)
Baby Octopus Chargrilled with Moroccan Spices (page 125)
Pumpkin and Eggplant Tagine with Whole
Green Chillies (page 146)

Pickled Green Chillies

1 kg (2 lb) long green chillies
60 g (2 oz) sea salt
700 ml (23 fl oz) water
500 ml (16 fl oz) white wine vinegar
2 red bullet chillies
2 bay leaves
4 sprigs thyme

Pickled vegetables are an absolute must in any Middle Eastern pantry, where you will find gleaming bottles of everything from olives to turnips, eggplant, cucumbers and chillies. Pickles are an essential part of a mezze table, and are often served as an accompaniment to pre-prandial drinks, or in sandwiches, salads and other snacks. Aficionados of takeaway kebabs will often find these tangy pickled chillies tucked in with their falafel or doner kebabs.

Wash the green chillies well and dry thoroughly. Prick the chillies all over.

Dissolve the salt in the water and strain into a clean bowl. Add the vinegar to the brine.

Place the green and red chillies, bay leaves and thyme in a glass jar. Pour in the vinegar mixture and seal tightly. The chillies can be eaten after 5 days.

Makes 1 kg (2 lb)

WE USE PICKLED GREEN CHILLIES FOR:
Hungarian Mushroom Soup with Smoked Paprika
and Yoghurt Cheese (page 31)
Greek Rocket Salad (page 39)
Potato and Mussel Salad with Harissa Dressing (page 41)
Grilled Turkish Bread and Vegetable Salad (page 45)
Waxy Potato Salad with Chickpeas and Chorizo (page 49)
Greek Leek Croquettes (page 53)
Eggplant Rice Pilaf with Hilbeh and Yoghurt (page 71)
Lentils and Rice with Caramelised Onions (page 76)
Duck Shish Kebab (page 102)
Shish Kifte (page 108)
Tuna Kibbeh with Pickled Vegetables
and Fresh Mint (page 122)

Eggplant Jam

6 medium-sized eggplant
(aubergine), cut into
2 cm (³/4 in) dice

salt

150 ml (5 fl oz) olive oil

4 small purple onions, sliced finely

1 tablespoon ground cumin

1 teaspoon ground coriander

¹/2 teaspoon white pepper

3 bullet chillies, seeded,
scraped and finely diced

1 tablespoon sherry or
white wine vinegar

2 tablespoons unsalted butter

A lovely lush, sweet, soft, sticky mess of eggplant and onions that is an absolute essential in the Malouf kitchen. The cumin, coriander and chilli give the jam an almost Indian touch, but it is wonderful with all kinds of dishes, from tagines to cold meats or in sandwiches. We also use it as a stuffing, mixed with cooked rice, in poultry dishes.

Put the eggplant into a colander and sprinkle lightly with salt. This draws out the moisture and reduces the amount of oil they absorb during cooking. Leave for 20 minutes. When ready to use, rinse and pat dry with kitchen paper.

Heat the oil in large heavy-based pot and fry the eggplant until golden brown. (You may need to do this in two batches.) Remove from the oil and drain on kitchen paper. Fry the onions in the remaining oil – cook them slowly so that they soften down and turn translucent, but don't colour.

Add the spices and chillies to the onions and mix well. Tip the eggplant back into the pan and stir to combine. Keep the heat low and cook the jam very slowly for about 30 minutes, by which time the eggplant will have melted down into a jammy mass. Taste it for seasoning then splash in the vinegar and butter and stir.

Tip into a colander over the sink and leave to sit for 5 minutes. This allows some of the oil to drain away. Pour into a jar and refrigerate. It will last for a couple of weeks. Makes 425 g (4 oz)

SERVE EGGPLANT JAM WITH:
Cheese-stuffed Kataifi (page 56)
Wild Mushroom Couscous with Fiore di Latte (page 80)
Giant Couscous (page 81)
Cracked Wheat Pilaf with Wild Mushrooms
and Sour Cream (page 84)
Crisp Fried Goat's Cheese Ravioli (page 85)
Chicken Baked with Almond Crumbs (page 88)
Chicken Schnitzel Fried in Cumin Butter (page 89)
Roast Quail Stuffed with Rice and Nuts (page 97)
Pork Roasted with Black Pepper and Cinnamon (page 113)

soups

Chicken Soup with Egg and Lemon and Bird's Nest Pasta

STOCK

1 large chicken, about 1 kg (2 lb)

1 kg (2 lb) chicken bones

2 onions, roughly diced

2 sticks celery, roughly diced

1 medium-sized leek,
white part only, roughly diced

2 cloves garlic, halved

1 cinnamon stick

1 teaspoon white peppercorns

2 bay leaves

peel of 1/2 lemon

1/4 teaspoon allspice

SOUP

250 g (8 oz) dried 'bird's nest'
vermicelli noodles

5 egg yolks

juice of 1 lemon

extra virgin olive oil

1 teaspoon cinnamon

1 teaspoon sweet paprika

salt and pepper

In essence, this is a kind of chicken noodle soup with a twist, based on a simple chicken broth flavoured with lemon and cinnamon that Greg's mother used to make. It's not one of those hearty all-in-one meal types of soups, but rather a light broth that is restorative and uplifting in the way of all good chicken soups.

A good stock requires a certain degree of love and attention, but is also intensely rewarding. It's not so much about effort or difficulty, but more about the time, which is needed for the chicken bones to simmer away, imparting all their goodness to the broth. Once made, you can use the stock as a base for any other soup or dish that calls for chicken stock.

Wash the chicken and bones and put them into a 5 litre cooking pot. Pour over enough water to completely cover and bring to the boil. Skim away the scum, add the vegetables and bring it back to the boil. Add the cinnamon, peppercorns, bay leaves, lemon peel and allspice. Simmer very gently for 1 1/2 hours, uncovered. Skim off any scum that forms on the surface regularly. Carefully lift out the chicken. Set aside.

Let the stock simmer gently for another hour. At the end of the cooking time, the liquid will have reduced quite substantially and you will have around 2 litres (4 pints) stock. Very carefully ladle the liquid into a fine sieve. The less you disturb the bones and vegetables in the process the clearer the final broth will be. If you like, you can now chill or freeze this stock for future use.

To make the soup, pull the meat off the chicken, throwing away the bones and skin, and tear the flesh into smallish pieces.

Slowly bring 1.5 litres (3 pints) of the chicken stock to the boil, season to taste, then lower the heat to a very low simmer. In a separate pot, cook the noodles in boiling salted water until they are tender. Try to keep the little nest shapes intact.

In a mixing bowl, whisk together the eggs and lemon juice. Ladle a spoonful of the hot stock into the egg mixture, stir it well, then pour the egg mixture into the barely simmering stock, whisking well all the time. Cook gently over a low heat until the soup gradually starts to thicken. Taste and adjust the seasoning if necessary – it should be fragrant, refreshing and lemony, with a luscious velvety-smooth texture.

Divide the chicken flesh between 6 serving bowls, and place a nest of noodles on top. Remove the soup from the heat and ladle over the chicken and noodles. To serve, drizzle with a little extra virgin olive oil and sprinkle with the cinnamon and paprika. For an extra hit of lemon, add some finely shredded Preserved Lemon (see pages 20–1).

SERVES 6

Cock-a-Leekie with Dates and Croque Monsieur

SOUP

50 ml (1¹/₂ fl oz) olive oil

4 leeks, white only, shredded

100 ml (3¹/₂ fl oz) sherry

¹/₂ teaspoon allspice

¹/₂ teaspoon grated nutmeg

¹/₂ teaspoon ground ginger

salt

¹/₄ teaspoon ground white pepper

6 fresh dates, seeded and diced

1.5 litres (3 pints) Chicken Stock (see page 26)

1 tablespoon finely chopped parsley

CROQUES MONSIEURS

12 slices white bread, crusts removed

softened butter

Dijon mustard

6 slices good-quality leg ham

250 g (8 oz) gruyère cheese, grated

50 g (1¹/₂ oz) unsalted butter

50 ml (1¹/₂ fl oz) olive oil

Let's be honest, there's nothing remotely Middle Eastern about Scotland's favourite soup! Although he turned his nose up at the idea of the prunes, which feature in the original, Greg did like the idea of popping dried fruit into a savoury soup – it's a theme that is popular all around the Middle East and in North Africa.

After a few days mulling it over, he came up with the following wonderfully fragrant soup, which uses fresh dates to add little nuggets of toffee sweetness.

The accompanying fried cheese sandwiches are also a real winner. If you have a toasted sandwich maker, then the *croques monsieurs* are a doddle to make. Otherwise you can fry them for a lovely rich toasty crust. If you are diet-conscious, plain old toasting would be fine too.

To make the soup, heat the olive oil in a large saucepan and lightly sauté the leeks for a few minutes until they soften. Raise the heat and add the sherry, then let it all bubble away for a minute or two. Stir in the spices, salt and pepper and the dates. Add the chicken stock and bring to the boil. Lower the heat and simmer very gently for 10–15 minutes, until the leeks are nice and tender and the dates and spices have infused their sweetness to the soup.

Towards the end of the cooking time, make the *croques monsieurs*. Butter the bread and spread with mustard. Lay on the ham and plenty of cheese and press the top slice of bread on firmly. Melt the butter and oil together in a frying pan and fry the sandwiches on both sides until they are golden brown.

When ready to serve, taste the soup and adjust the seasoning as necessary. Ladle into serving bowls and sprinkle with parsley. Serve with the *croques monsieurs*, wrapped in a natty little napkin if you like!

SERVES 6

Green Gazpacho
with Coriander

2 thick slices stale white bread, cubed

2 cloves garlic, roughly chopped

1 teaspoon sea salt

2 large green peppers, seeded and roughly chopped

2 green (or unripe) tomatoes, skinned, seeded and roughly chopped

1 soft-leaved lettuce, like a butter lettuce

3 spring onions (scallions)

1 cup coriander (cilantro), roots removed

5 tablespoons extra virgin olive oil

4 tablespoons sherry vinegar

1/4 teaspoon cayenne pepper

500 ml (16 fl oz) icy-cold water

juice of 1/2 lemon

finely diced cucumber or pomegranate seeds (optional)

extra virgin olive oil

An unusual all-green version of the popular Spanish soup, which uses coriander to add a citrussy zing. The key thing with gazpacho is that it must be served very well chilled. What you absolutely don't want is the style of gazpacho that is so often served up in restaurants: a thin watery vegetable juice dotted with semi-melted bits of floating ice. Gazpacho is at its most refreshing and best when it is thick and creamy and cold, cold, cold.

Soak the bread briefly in a little water, then squeeze lightly. Put the bread into a food processor with the garlic and salt and pulse until well mixed. Add the green peppers and blitz everything to as smooth a purée as you can. Then, with the motor running, add the tomatoes, followed by the lettuce, spring onions and coriander, making sure that everything is well and truly incorporated. Finally, mix in the olive oil, vinegar and cayenne pepper. Pour the soup base into a container, cover and refrigerate (or freeze) until icy-cold.

When you want to serve it, add the iced water and lemon juice, taste and add more salt if necessary. Serve garnished with finely diced cucumber or pomegranate seeds and a drizzle of your best extra virgin olive oil. A handful of coriander leaves would also look pretty.

SERVES 6

Fennel Soup with Lemon and Cinnamon

60 ml (2 fl oz) olive oil

2 onions, sliced

2 cloves garlic, roughly chopped

2 leeks, roughly chopped

3 large bulbs fennel, sliced

2 potatoes, peeled and cut into chunks

1.5 litres (3 pints) Chicken Stock (see page 26)

1 cinnamon stick

peel of $\frac{1}{2}$ lemon

$\frac{1}{2}$ teaspoon allspice

2 bay leaves

salt and pepper

2 egg yolks

150 ml (5 fl oz) thickened cream

juice of 2 lemons

extra virgin olive oil

1 teaspoon ground cinnamon

1 tablespoon roughly chopped parsley

We love fennel for its sweetness and subtle aniseed flavour. Here, it is transformed into a delightful lemony soup with a comforting cinnamon fragrance. It is made a little richer by adding cream and egg yolks towards the end of the cooking.

Heat the oil in a large heavy-based saucepan and sauté the onions, garlic, leeks and fennel for a few minutes until they soften. Add the potatoes and chicken stock, then the cinnamon stick, lemon peel, allspice and bay leaves. Bring to the boil, then lower the heat and simmer gently for 20 minutes. Remove and discard the cinnamon stick, lemon peel and bay leaves, and season to taste with salt and pepper.

In a separate bowl, mix the egg yolks with the cream, then ladle in a spoonful of the hot soup. Whisk together well, then tip the egg mixture into the soup. Slowly return the soup to just below boiling, stirring it all the time. Remove from the heat and adjust the seasoning, with extra salt and pepper and the lemon juice.

As you serve, drizzle each bowl with extra virgin olive oil and sprinkle with a little cinnamon and parsley.

SERVES 6

Hungarian Mushroom Soup with Smoked Paprika and Yoghurt Cheese

YOGHURT CHEESE

1 clove garlic

1 teaspoon sea salt

500 g (1 lb) plain yoghurt

SOUP

80 ml (2$\frac{1}{2}$ fl oz) olive oil

1 large onion, diced

1 stick celery, diced

1 medium-sized carrot, diced

1 clove garlic, chopped

1 bullet chilli, seeded, scraped and roughly chopped

1 teaspoon thyme leaves

2 bay leaves

1 tablespoon sweet paprika

1 kg (2 lb) field mushrooms, sliced

a splash of sherry

2 medium-sized potatoes, peeled and diced

2 litres (4 pints) water or vegetable stock

1 teaspoon salt

1 teaspoon smoked paprika

We love this thick hearty soup, rich and smoky with paprika and hot with a chilli-buzz. Greg was inspired to create this dish after a trip to Budapest while he was working in Austria. Chock-full of mushrooms and vegetables, it is like a goulash, with the creamy yoghurt cheese making a nice (and slightly healthier) change from the more traditional sour cream.

To make the yoghurt cheese, first crush the garlic and salt to a smooth paste and stir into the yoghurt. Spoon into a clean muslin square or tea-towel, tie the four corners together and suspend the bundle from a wooden spoon over a deep bowl. Put it in the refrigerator and allow it to drain for 6 hours or overnight.

To make the soup, heat the oil in a large heavy-based saucepan, then add the onion, celery, carrot and garlic, and sauté for a few minutes until they soften. Add the chilli, thyme, bay leaves, sweet paprika and the mushrooms and stir everything around well. Raise the heat and pour in a splash of sherry. Then add the potatoes and stock, season with the salt and bring to the boil. Lower the heat and simmer for 20–30 minutes, until the potatoes are tender.

When you are ready to serve, taste and adjust the seasoning if necessary. Ladle the soup into bowls and top with a blob of yoghurt cheese and a dusting of smoked paprika.

SERVES 6

Mussel Mulligatawny with Preserved Lemon Risotto

1.5 kg (3 lb) mussels

60 ml (2 fl oz) olive oil

1 onion, finely chopped

1 leek, white part only, finely chopped

1 clove garlic, finely chopped

100 ml (3½ fl oz) white wine

1 teaspoon turmeric

1 teaspoon chilli powder

1 teaspoon ground coriander

1 teaspoon ground cumin

½ teaspoon ground ginger

⅓ cup parsley, roughly chopped

1 tablespoon chopped celery leaves (from the heart)

200 ml (7 fl oz) thickened cream

½ recipe Preserved Lemon Risotto (see page 70)

The liquor released by mussels during the cooking process is one of the best things about them, and here it provides the base for a wonderful mulligatawny soup. This is a fabulous dish, full of creamy curry flavours, and a touch of chilli heat. Rice, the traditional accompaniment to Asian curries, is also terrific in soups, turning them into more of a meal. A spoonful of preserved lemon risotto works perfectly in this soup, or, if you don't fancy making risotto especially for this dish, then any leftover rice you might have hanging around in the fridge will do. Just stir through some diced preserved lemon, celery leaves and a knob of butter as you warm it.

This soup would be delicious as a starter on a cold evening, but is also hearty enough to be eaten on its own as a supper or lunch dish.

Scrub the mussels clean and pull away the beards (throw away any that refuse to close after a sharp tap).

Heat the oil in a large heavy-based cooking pot and add the onion, leek and garlic. Stir around over a medium heat for a few minutes, then tip in the mussels and shake the pan to move them around over the heat. Pour in the wine, cover the pan, turn up the heat and steam for 3–4 minutes. Shake the pan vigorously from time to time.

Remove the lid from the pan and stir the mussels around well. Most should have opened, but if there are still many that remain closed, stir them around, then put the lid back on and steam them for a further 2 minutes. Take the pan off the heat and remove the mussels from their shells, discarding any that haven't opened. Return the mussel meat to the pan.

Put the pan back on the heat, and add the spices, parsley, celery leaves and cream. Bring to the boil and mix everything well.

When ready to serve, place a small mound of risotto into each soup bowl and spoon the mussels, vegetables and lovely fragrant creamy juices around.

SERVES 4 AS A GENEROUS STARTER OR LIGHT LUNCH DISH

Devilled Green Lentil Soup with Candied Ham Hock

50 ml (1½ fl oz) olive oil

2 onions, sliced

2 cloves garlic, chopped

1 tablespoon Tabil (see page 9) or 2 bullet chillies, seeded, scraped and roughly chopped

500 g (1 lb) green lentils

3 litres (6 pints) chicken or vegetable stock

1 small smoked ham hock

2 sprigs thyme

2 sprigs rosemary

1 bay leaf

1 teaspoon crushed white peppercorns

zest and juice of 2 lemons

1 teaspoon allspice

1 tablespoon honey

salt

1 tablespoon raw sugar

extra virgin olive oil

Lentils are the perfect vehicle for spices and, as here, a devilish chilli heat. They provide a smooth starchy base that is intensely comforting and filling. Beneath the buzz of the chilli, the honey adds a sweet base note that is echoed by the candied ham hock. This soup is very filling, which makes it ideal as a supper or lunch dish on a cold wintry day with some hot crusty bread.

Heat the olive oil in a large cooking pot and sauté the onions, garlic and chillies until they soften. Add the lentils and stir around well. Now pour on the stock and add the remaining ingredients, except the salt and sugar. Bring to the boil, then lower the heat and simmer gently for 1½–2 hours, until the lentils are very tender and the ham is cooked through. Remove the hock from the soup and when it is cool enough to handle, remove the skin. Pull the flesh off the bone, shred roughly, and set aside.

Remove and discard the thyme, rosemary and bay leaf. Purée the soup in a food processor or blender, then taste and add salt as necessary – if it is very thick, you may like to thin it down with a little water or stock.

When you are ready to serve, preheat the grill (broiler) to its hottest temperature. Spread the shredded ham out on a baking sheet and sprinkle over the sugar. Place under the grill until the sugar caramelises and the ham begins to crisp up.

Ladle the soup into serving bowls and garnish with the candied ham and a drizzle of extra virgin olive oil.

SERVES 6

Tunisian Lamb Soup with Almonds and Fenugreek

SOUP

4 lamb shanks

salt and pepper

80 ml (2½ fl oz) olive oil

2 cloves garlic, peeled

1 cinnamon stick

1 bay leaf

1 large leek, washed
and halved lengthways

a few sprigs of fresh thyme

2 litres (4 pints) Chicken Stock
(see page 26) or water

50 ml (1½ fl oz) olive oil

1 large brown
onion, finely diced

2 cloves garlic, finely chopped

1 teaspoon ground cumin

1 teaspoon ground turmeric

1 teaspoon ground ginger

1 teaspoon ground cinnamon

10 threads saffron, lightly roasted
and crushed

1 tablespoon honey

1 x 400 g (14 oz) can
crushed tomatoes

18 pickling onions, peeled

100 g (3½ oz) cooked chickpeas
or 1 x 400 g (14 oz) can
chickpeas, drained

2 tablespoons Hilbeh
(see page 17)

60 g (2 oz) flaked almonds, fried
until golden brown

Lamb shanks are one of our favourite cuts. Although they need long, slow cooking, they don't require much in the way of attention once they are simmering away. Here, they make a wonderfully fragrant and filling soup with warm, sweet undertones from the honey and cinnamon. Finish with a swirl of exotic green hilbeh and crunchy golden almonds and serve with wedges of lemon and some warm pitta bread.

To make the soup, season the lamb shanks with salt and pepper. Heat the oil in a large heavy-based pot and brown the shanks, turning them so they colour evenly. Lower the heat, and drain away any burnt fat. Add the garlic, cinnamon, bay leaf, leek and thyme. Pour on the stock or water and bring to the boil. Lower the heat and simmer very gently for 2 hours, uncovered. Skim off any fat and scum that forms on the surface from time to time. You may need to top up with extra stock too.

In a medium-sized pot, heat the oil and sauté the onion and garlic over a low heat until they soften. Add the spices and cook for a further 5 minutes. Then add the honey, tomatoes, onions and chickpeas and strain in the liquid from the pot of lamb shanks. Simmer gently for 20–30 minutes.

Remove the meat from the shanks, discarding any fat and sinew. Roughly shred the meat and add to the soup. Return to a gentle boil and taste, adjusting the seasoning if necessary.

To serve, ladle the soup into bowls, swirl in a teaspoon of hilbeh and sprinkle with almonds.

SERVES 6

salads

Couscous Salad with Watercress and Avocado

SALAD

1 tablespoon extra
virgin olive oil

100 ml (3½ fl oz) water

200 g (7 oz) couscous

salt

1 avocado, cut into
1 cm (½ in) dice

1 bunch watercress,
leaves picked
(about ¾ cup)

4 spring onions
(scallions), finely chopped

½ cup mint leaves, shredded

DRESSING

juice of 1 lime

60 ml (2 fl oz) extra
virgin olive oil

½ teaspoon ground cinnamon

½ teaspoon allspice

¼ teaspoon chilli powder

1 teaspoon Dijon mustard

Just to show its versatility, why not try using couscous in a cold tabbouleh-like salad? Couscous is lighter and fluffier than the traditional and nuttier cracked wheat (burghul), although both work well in this dish. The resulting very pretty, green-flecked grainy salad is a delicious accompaniment to a simple piece of grilled fish or chicken.

Sprinkle the oil and water onto the couscous and rub it between your fingers for a few minutes until all the grains are coated. Leave to sit for 20 minutes so the grains start to absorb the moisture and swell. Then take a fork and work through the couscous to break down any lumps.

Tip the couscous into a steamer lined with a tea towel and seal the sides with a tea towel or cling film. Steam for 20–30 minutes, uncovered, over rapid boiling water until the couscous grains soften and become fluffy. Remove from the heat and tip into a heatproof serving bowl. Gently fork through the grains until they run smoothly and season with salt. Allow to cool completely.

To make the dressing, combine the lime juice and olive oil. Add the spices and mustard and whisk everything together well.

Place the couscous in a large bowl with the avocado, watercress, spring onions and mint. Pour on the dressing, lightly season, toss and serve.

SERVES 4

Greek Rocket Salad

8 radishes, cut into wedges

3 tomatoes, cut into wedges

2 Lebanese cucumbers, cut into chunky lengths

1 purple onion, sliced

60 g (2 oz) black olives

50 g (1½ oz) wild rocket (arugula)

1 tablespoon dried oregano

80 g (2½ oz) good quality fetta

DRESSING

60 ml (2 fl oz) extra virgin olive oil

2 tablespoons white wine vinegar

1 teaspoon pomegranate molasses

Greek salads are chock-full of robust flavours so peppery rocket works well. It is increasingly easy to get good quality wild rocket these days, which has a strong, vital flavour. This is a fairly traditional combination of chunky-cut salad vegetables, salty olives and cheese and oregano. A splash of syrupy pomegranate molasses in the dressing adds a hint of dark sweet-sourness.

Put all the salad ingredients, except the fetta and oregano, into a mixing bowl. Sprinkle over the oregano.

To make the dressing, whisk together the olive oil, vinegar, pomegranate molasses and season with salt and pepper.

Pour the dressing over the salad and mix well. Crumble the fetta over the salad and fold it through gently, aiming to maintain the shape of each chunk, rather than have it mush down to a paste.

SERVES 4

Shredded Carrot Salad

2 large carrots, coarsely grated

DRESSING

1 clove garlic, crushed with ½ teaspoon sea salt

¼ teaspoon ground cinnamon

¼ teaspoon ground cumin

¼ teaspoon paprika

¼ teaspoon chilli powder

juice of 1 large lemon

a drizzle of honey

2 tablespoons extra virgin olive oil

splash of orange-blossom water (optional)

When we were in Morocco, a variation on the carrot salad appeared on just about every restaurant and café menu. Often we found them cloying, sweetened as they were with sugar, cinnamon and orange-blossom water. In our view, carrots have plenty of their own natural sweetness, so all we add is a drizzle of honey for flavour. All they really need is a touch of spice and chilli and a dash of lemon juice to make a very exotic yet still refreshing salad.

To make the dressing, put all the ingredients into a clean jar and shake everything together vigorously until well combined.

Tip over the carrots, taste and adjust seasoning if necessary. And that's it!

SERVES 4 AS AN ACCOMPANIMENT OR AS PART OF A MEZZE SELECTION

Potato and Mussel Salad with Harissa Dressing

MUSSELS

1.5 kg (3 lb) mussels

1 tablespoon olive oil

1 small onion, finely sliced

1 stick celery, roughly chopped

2 cloves garlic, roughly chopped

1 bay leaf

100 ml (3½ fl oz) white wine

SALAD

2 large waxy potatoes

6 spring onions (scallions)

2 Pickled Green Chillies (optional, see page 23), seeded and shredded

2 medium-sized tomatoes, seeded and finely diced

⅓ cup parsley, roughly chopped

⅓ cup coriander (cilantro), roughly chopped

100 ml (3½ fl oz) good quality mayonnaise

1 tablespoon Red Harissa (see page 16)

juice of ½ lemon

1 tablespoon extra virgin olive oil

salt and pepper

Potato salads are incredibly versatile, their starchiness providing the perfect foil for all sorts of ingredients. The trick is to pour on the dressing while the potatoes are still warm, so that they drink up all the added flavours. This salad would be great as part of a mezze selection, or as a side dish at a barbecue or picnic.

Scrub the mussels clean of any sand and dirt, and pull away the beards.

In a heavy-based pot, heat the oil and sauté the onion, celery and garlic until they just start to soften. Add the mussels and wine, cover the pan and steam on high heat for 2 minutes. Stir the mussels around well, and steam for a further 2 minutes. Remove the pan from the heat and leave them covered to steam for another minute or so. Strain off the cooking liquor and reserve. Discard the aromatics and any of the mussels that remain unopened. Remove the mussels from their shells and leave the meat with a little of the cooking liquor until ready to assemble the salad.

Peel the potatoes and cut them into neat smallish dice. Steam for about 10 minutes, or until tender. While the potatoes are cooking, prepare the remaining salad ingredients, and mix the harissa with the mayonnaise to make a dressing.

When the potatoes are cooked, tip them into a large mixing bowl and, while they are still hot, sprinkle over the lemon juice and olive oil, salt and pepper, and mix gently so that they absorb the flavours. Next add the spring onions, chillies, tomatoes, parsley, coriander and the mussels, along with a little bit of their juice.

Pour on the harissa dressing and use your hands to mix everything together gently. Serve with a glass of chilled sauvignon blanc and a crusty baguette.

SERVES 4

Eggplant Salad with Tahini–Yoghurt Dressing

2 eggplant (aubergine)

salt

100 ml (3½ fl oz) olive oil

150 ml (5 fl oz) Tahini–Yoghurt Sauce (see page 12)

⅓ cup parsley leaves

½ small purple onion, diced

1 tomato, diced

1 tablespoon extra virgin olive oil

salt and pepper

sumac

Most people are acquainted with tahini – the Middle Eastern paste made from crushed sesame seeds – through its use in popular dips such as hummus and baba ghanoush. But it is also common to find it thinned down with water and used as a base for sauces. In this, its simplest form, it can often be a little bitter for western palates. But partnered with creamy yoghurt, and flavoured with a little garlic and lemon juice, it becomes divinely smooth and creamy, with a mysterious earthy flavour.

Tahini–yoghurt dressings are frequently served with cold baked fish, or with grilled meats or even felafel. In this substantial salad, the rich oiliness of eggplant is matched with the dark flavours of nutty tahini, and sharpened by the lemony-sourness of yoghurt.

Cut the eggplant in half and then into long, chip-like wedges. Put them in a colander and sprinkle the flesh with salt. After 20 minutes rinse under cold water and pat dry with kitchen paper.

Fry the eggplant in the oil, turning from time to time, until they are coloured a rich deep-golden brown. Drain on kitchen paper.

Arrange the eggplant on a serving plate and drizzle generously with the dressing. In a separate bowl, combine the parsley, onion and tomato with the tablespoon of olive oil. Season with salt and pepper and scatter loosely over the eggplant. Serve sprinkled with sumac and an extra drizzle of extra virgin olive oil.

SERVES 4

Tabbouleh with Roasted Walnuts

70 g (2¼ oz) walnuts

2 bunches flat-leaf parsley, leaves only

½ bunch mint, finely shredded

1 large purple onion, finely chopped

4 medium-sized tomatoes, finely diced

juice of 2 lemons

½ teaspoon allspice

⅓ teaspoon ground cinnamon

½ teaspoon salt

½ teaspoon pepper

100–120 ml (3½–4 fl oz) olive oil

Tabbouleh is undoubtedly one of our favourite salads (despite its depressingly soggy ubiquity), with its simple focus on fresh flavours and textures. Here, roasted walnuts add a lovely nutty flavour and crunch to the traditional version. By all means roast the walnuts and prepare the individual vegetables and herbs ahead of time. But don't mix in the lemon juice and oil until the very last moment or the whole thing will go mushy.

Preheat the oven to 160°C 325°F).

Spread the walnuts out on a baking sheet and put it in the oven for 8–10 minutes. After 4 minutes, shake the tray around so that the nuts colour evenly. Remove the tray from the oven and tip the nuts into a tea-towel. Rub them vigorously between your hands to remove as much of the papery brown skin as you can. Chop the nuts finely to the texture of coarse breadcrumbs. Sieve to remove as much of the dust as you can.

Put the parsley, mint, onion, tomatoes and walnuts into a large bowl. Add the remaining ingredients and mix well with your hands. Taste and adjust the seasoning if necessary.

SERVES 8–10

Grilled Turkish Bread and Vegetable Salad

3 tomatoes, cut into large dice

2 Lebanese cucumbers, cut into large dice

2 salad onions, sliced

100 g (3½ oz) cooked lima beans, skinned

60 g (2 oz) big black olives

2 tablespoons shredded parsley leaves

around a quarter of a big loaf of flat Turkish bread

2 tablespoons extra virgin olive oil

1 clove garlic, crushed with ½ teaspoon sea salt

juice of 1 lemon

60 ml (2 fl oz) extra virgin olive oil, extra

1 tablespoon toasted sesame seeds

This is a big-flavoured hearty salad, filling enough to serve as a first course or as a lunch dish in its own right. Frying the bread makes it richer, lusher, and oilier and heavier on the calories. If this bothers you, feel free to treat it more like bruschetta, and merely brush it with a little oil and grill it.

Lima beans make a lovely nutty, buttery addition to any salad and they don't take as long to prepare as some pulses. Soak them in hot water for half an hour and then cook in plenty of unsalted simmering water until they are tender. Amazingly, given their size, this only takes 20–30 minutes.

Put the tomatoes, cucumbers, onions, lima beans, olives and parsley in a large mixing bowl.

Split the Turkish bread in half and cut into 2 cm (¾ in) pieces. Brush each little piece with the oil and toast under a hot grill. Alternatively, you can fry the bread in olive oil.

Whisk the garlic paste into the lemon juice and the 60 ml olive oil to make a dressing. Sprinkle sesame seeds over the salad, then toss in the grilled bread. Pour on the dressing and mix everything together well. Serve immediately so the bread doesn't go soggy.

SERVES 4

Prawn Fattouche with Turkish Bread

1 tablespoon sumac

1 medium-sized purple onion, finely sliced

¼ teaspoon allspice

¼ teaspoon pepper

4 cos lettuce leaves, washed and dried

4 radishes, thickly sliced

2 tomatoes, ripe but firm, roughly diced

2 Lebanese cucumbers, cut into chunky dice

½ cup parsley leaves, roughly chopped

⅓ cup mint leaves, roughly chopped (or 1 tablespoon dried mint)

around a quarter of a big loaf of flat Turkish bread

60 g (2 oz) butter

60 ml (2 fl oz) olive oil

1 teaspoon Ras al Hanout (see page 3)

400 g (14 oz) small whole raw prawns (shrimps)

2 tablespoons olive oil

DRESSING
1 clove garlic, crushed with 1 teaspoon sea salt

juice of 1 lemon

3 tablespoons extra virgin olive oil

1 tablespoon white wine vinegar

Fattouche is the classic Lebanese garden salad, made more filling with the addition of fried Arabic bread. There isn't anything refined about fattouche, so use whatever is best and freshest from your garden (or fridge). The addition of prawns makes it into a real meal. But rather than the monster tiger or king prawns, use the little tasty ones that you cook whole, and eat shell, head and all – if you are game!

All prawns these days are frozen, except for farmed tiger prawns which some better fishmongers sell fresh. When buying, check the heads for any black oxidised spots. These are a sign that they have been poorly handled and likely to be old and have been sitting defrosted on the fishmonger's slab for too long. Ideally you should buy them still frozen and defrost them yourself at home.

Soak the sumac in cold water for a few minutes and remove any husks that float to the surface. Put the onion into a small bowl with the sumac, allspice and pepper and rub everything together well.

Cut the cos leaves crossways into 3 cm (1¼ in) strips. Put them in a large mixing bowl with the radishes, tomatoes, cucumbers and herbs.

To make the dressing, whisk the garlic paste with the lemon juice, extra virgin olive oil and white wine vinegar.

Split the Turkish bread and cut into 2 cm (¾ in) pieces. Melt the butter and oil in a frying pan until foaming, and fry the bread in two batches until golden brown. Remove with a slotted spoon and drain on kitchen paper.

Sprinkle the ras al hanout over the prawns and stir them around to coat well. Heat the oil in a frying pan or wok. Tip in half the prawns and fry for 2 minutes, stirring constantly, until they turn a pretty pink and just lose their translucency. Repeat with the remainder.

When you are ready to serve, add the spiced onions and fried Turkish bread pieces to the other salad ingredients, pour on the dressing and mix everything together well. Divide the salad among 4 plates and top with the prawns. Eat straight away.

SERVES 4

Asparagus with Grilled Haloumi and Honey-seared Witlof

DRESSING

2 tablespoons walnut oil

2 tablespoons olive oil

a few drops of sesame oil

2 tablespoons champagne or white wine vinegar

juice of 1/2 lemon

salt and pepper

SALAD

250 g (8 oz) white asparagus

1 tablespoon honey

a pinch of ground cardamom

freshly ground black pepper

a splash of orange-blossom water

2 tablespoons olive oil

4 witlof, halved and core removed

1 bunch watercress (or a handful of rocket/arugula leaves), leaves picked (about 3/4 cup)

1 purple onion, finely sliced

60 g (2 oz) walnuts, roasted and skins rubbed away

HALOUMI

2 tablespoons olive oil

1 block Cypriot haloumi cheese, about 200 g (7 oz), soaked in cold water for 30 minutes to remove excess salt

plain flour for dusting

1/2 lemon

1/2 teaspoon chopped thyme leaves

This is one of the prettiest salads you can imagine, in shades of white and the palest of pale greens. It isn't really a salad you fling together at the last minute, but rather, is carefully composed of sophisticated flavours: delicate sweet asparagus, the salty tang of haloumi and the astringency of witlof. If possible, try to get white asparagus for this dish. It has a lovely delicate flavour, and these days is quite easy to find. Some people complain that they find witlof too bitter, but here it is sautéed with honey, fragrant cardamom and orange-blossom water, which mellows it out in the mouth.

To make the dressing, whisk all the ingredients together and season lightly.

To make the salad, snap the woody ends off the asparagus and peel them up to the top. Drop them into boiling salted water and cook for 10 minutes, or until tender. Refresh them in cold water and cut each spear in half on an angle.

Mix the honey with the cardamom, pepper and orange-blossom water. Heat the oil in a frying pan and sear the witlof, cut side down first. Turn and sear the other side. Brush the cut side with the honey glaze, then turn back over and cook for a couples of minutes until the honey caramelises. Keep the pieces moving in the pan and add a splash of water if it looks as if the honey will burn. Remove from the heat and tip into a large mixing bowl.

Add the watercress, onion, walnuts and asparagus and dress with half the dressing. Divide the salad among 4 plates.

Heat the oil in a frying pan. Cut the haloumi into 8 slices and dust with a little flour. When the oil in the pan is almost smoking hot, add the cheese and fry them for 30 seconds on each side, until they are a rich golden brown. At the end of the frying, squeeze over the lemon juice and sprinkle with the chopped thyme.

Place 2 slices of hot haloumi on top of each mound of salad and drizzle the remaining dressing around the plate.

SERVES 4

Waxy Potato Salad with Chickpeas and Chorizo

DRESSING

1 tablespoon fennel seeds, lightly roasted and crushed

1 tablespoon coriander seeds, lightly roasted and crushed

4 shallots, finely diced

1 teaspoon white peppercorns, crushed

1 tablespoon thyme leaves

12 strands saffron

a drizzle of honey

2 tablespoons white wine vinegar

80 ml (2½ fl oz) extra virgin olive oil

juice of ½ lemon

2 large, mild red chillies, seeded, scraped and roughly chopped

SALAD

300 g (10 oz) waxy potatoes

100 g (3½ oz) cooked chickpeas (garbanzo)

2 tablespoons olive oil

160 g (5⅓ oz) semi-dried chorizo sausages, sliced thickly

100 g (3½ oz) frisée lettuce or baby curly endive

1 cup coriander (cilantro) leaves, roughly chopped

2 medium-soft boiled eggs, peeled and halved

We love potato salads, and we love thick slices of spicy chorizo, the oily, orange Spanish sausage. All that is needed is some bitter salad leaves and a good, sharp dressing, to make what is for us, the perfect salad. Top with halves of softly oozing boiled eggs and you have an intensely flavourful and satisfying lunch or supper dish.

To make the dressing, put all the ingredients in a large mixing bowl and allow them to infuse for at least an hour.

To make the salad, peel and boil the potatoes until they are tender. Dice. Put the chickpeas in a pan of water and bring to the boil so they warm through. Drain well, and mix with the potatoes. While they are still warm, pour over the dressing and stir gently.

Heat the olive oil in a frying pan and sauté the chorizo for a minute on each side to warm through. Add the chorizo and the oil from the pan, the lettuce and coriander to the potatoes and chickpeas and mix together well. Serve the salad topped with the egg halves.

SERVES 4

Baby Spinach Leaves with Citrus Fruits and Crushed Pine Nuts

DRESSING

50 g (1½ oz) pine nuts, fried until golden brown

80 ml (2½ fl oz) extra virgin olive oil

a drizzle of honey

juice of ½ lemon

½ teaspoon sumac

200 g (7 oz) baby spinach leaves

50 g (1½ oz) radicchio leaves

1 lemon

1 lime

1 orange

1 avocado

1 purple onion, finely sliced

12 thin slices prosciutto

The good thing about salads is that all they are really about is easily combining flavours and textures that work well together – and you are limited only by your own imagination.

Here, we just love the salty pigginess of a good prosciutto, with the irony vitality of spinach, the slight bitterness of radicchio and the sour-sweetness of citrus fruits. And the crunchy nuttiness of toasted pine nuts as a garnish is the pièce de résistance. This salad actually works well with any citrus fruits: in season you could use pretty blood oranges, tangelos or ruby grapefruit.

To make the dressing, roughly crush the pine nuts in a mortar – you aren't aiming for a fine powder, but rather a crunchy mess of rough golden crumbs. Mix the pine nuts with the remaining dressing ingredients and whisk well.

Pick the stalks off the spinach leaves, then wash and dry thoroughly. Separate the radicchio leaves, wash and dry them well and then tear roughly into smallish pieces.

Peel the citrus fruits and, using a very sharp knife, carefully slice each segment out of its skin casing.

Peel the avocado, remove the pip and cut the flesh into medium-sized dice.

Put the leaves into a mixing bowl with the onion, avocado and fruit. Pour on the dressing and use your hands to mix everything together well. To serve, tip out onto a large serving plate and tuck the slices of prosciutto in among the salad.

SERVES 4

snacks

Haloumi Baked in Vine Leaves

16 hand-sized vine leaves,
fresh or preserved

2 blocks Cypriot haloumi, each
about 200 g (7 oz), soaked in
cold water for 1 hour

1 teaspoon sweet paprika

1/4 teaspoon chilli powder

16 thin slices prosciutto

2 tablespoons extra virgin
olive oil

2 tablespoons olive oil

lemon wedges

Haloumi is one of our favourite cheeses: it has a strange, almost rubbery texture and an addictive salty-sweet flavour. Eaten as is, it can be a little bland, but try dusting it with a little seasoned flour and frying or grilling it, Greek saganaki-style – it transforms into a delectable hot molten mess, with a lovely crisp-golden coating.

Here is another way of cooking it: wrapped in a layer of sweet prosciutto and tangy vine leaves, which char to a gorgeous crunch under the grill. If you're lucky enough to have a grape vine in your garden, or if you live near a vineyard, summer is the time to go harvesting. Fresh vine leaves have an incomparable citrus tang, without the often tinny-briny undertone that you find in the preserved ones. The latter are fine but need a thorough soaking and rinsing before you can use them.

If you are using preserved vine leaves, soak them well, then rinse and pat dry. Fresh vine leaves should first be blanched and refreshed.

After soaking the haloumi, pat dry and cut each block widthways into 8 fat slices.

Mix the chilli and paprika together and dust the cheese very lightly, then wrap with a slice of prosciutto.

Lay the vine leaves, vein side up, on the work surface. Lie the prosciutto-wrapped cheese block across the base of the leaf and splash on a drop of extra virgin olive oil. Roll the leaf over once, then fold in the sides and continue to roll into a neat little square parcel. Brush each parcel with a little olive oil and cook under a preheated very hot grill (broiler) for a few minutes on each side, or until the vine leaves start to colour and blister. Serve them straight from the grill with a squeeze of lemon.

SERVES 4 AS A STARTER OR SNACK

Greek Leek Croquettes

3 medium-sized leeks, white part only, finely sliced

1 clove garlic, finely sliced

1 tablespoon butter

200 ml (7 fl oz) Chicken Stock (see page 26)

1 bay leaf

salt and pepper

vegetable oil, for frying

PASTRY

1 litre (2 pints) water

250 g (8 oz) unsalted butter

500 g (1 lb) plain flour

1 teaspoon salt

a pinch of nutmeg

10 large eggs

250 g (8 oz) crumbled goat's cheese

50 g (1½ oz) grated parmesan

1 tablespoon finely chopped dill

The combination of dill and fresh cheese is very popular in the Middle East and Eastern Mediterranean. These airy golden choux balls are terrific with a glass of chilled bubbles as a pre-prandial snack. The quantities will make 30–40 croquettes.

Sauté the leek and garlic in the butter for a few minutes until they soften. Pour in the chicken stock and add the bay leaf, salt and pepper. Cut out a circle of greaseproof paper large enough to cover the leek mixture (this stops a skin forming as it slowly cooks down), lower the heat and cook very gently for 25 minutes, until the mixture has reduced down to a lovely soft mass. Remove the pan from the heat, and allow the mixture to cool. Peel away the paper and tip the leeks into a food processor. Pulse a few times to make a coarse purée. Set aside.

To make the pastry, put the water and butter in a large saucepan and slowly bring to the boil so that the butter completely dissolves. As the liquid boils, quickly add all the flour at once, and mix well with a wooden spoon to incorporate into the liquid. Continue cooking over a low heat for about 8 minutes, until the mixture is glossy and comes away from the sides of the pan in a smooth ball.

Tip the pastry into an electric mixer and beat for a few minutes on medium speed. Add the leek purée and then the eggs, one at a time, beating constantly. When all the eggs are incorporated, quickly mix in the cheeses and dill. Refrigerate the mixture until it is completely cold. (You can make the mixture up to a day ahead of time.)

Heat the oil in a deep-fryer or saucepan to 180°C (350°F), or until a cube of bread dropped in sizzles to the surface in about 30 seconds.

Shape the mixture into mini golfballs and deep-fry until they are golden brown and starting to split. Drain on kitchen paper and serve immediately.

SERVES 4

Salmon and Mint Briouats

FILLING

400 g (14 oz) raw salmon, skin removed and minced

1 tablespoon roughly chopped mint leaves

1 tablespoon roughly chopped coriander (cilantro) leaves

1 teaspoon dried mint

1 green chilli, seeded, scraped and roughly chopped

2 hard-boiled eggs, roughly chopped

1 tablespoon extra virgin olive oil

a drizzle of honey

salt and pepper

6 sheets prepared filo pastry

egg wash made from 1 egg and 1 teaspoon water

200 ml (7 fl oz) vegetable oil for shallow-frying

Briouats are the small triangular or rectangular pastries so popular in North Africa. They are called briouats in Morocco, briks in Tunisia and boureks in Algeria, and come stuffed with all kinds of filling, ranging from chicken to mashed tuna and egg to herbed cheese or vegetables.

These briouats are incredibly pretty, with their green-flecked pink filling, and the hint of chilli and fresh mint cut through the richness of the salmon. Prepare, cook and serve immediately, or, if it suits you better, you can make them ahead of time and freeze. The quantities here will make about 24 tiny briouats.

To make the filling, place all the ingredients in a large mixing bowl and combine thoroughly.

To make the briouats, lay a sheet of filo out on the work surface and cut lengthwise into quarters. Each piece will make one briouat. Take one strip and brush along its length with the egg wash. Place one tablespoon of the salmon mixture across the corner at one end of the pastry. Fold this corner up and over on the diagonal to make a triangle shape. Fold the triangle over, and continue in this fashion along the length of the pastry. You should end up with a neat little triangle-shaped pastry parcel. Seal any open edges with egg wash. Repeat with the remaining pastry and filling until you have about 24 briouats. At this stage, you can freeze the pastries if you like, but otherwise cook them immediately as the egg wash makes the pastry soggy.

When you are ready to eat, heat the oil in a frying pan or wok and fry the pastries, 3 at a time, until they are golden brown. They will probably take up to 2 minutes on each side. If they seem to be browning too fast, lower the heat, wait a few moments and try again.

Remove the briouats from the oil and drain on kitchen paper before serving. They are very tasty as is, hot from the pan, but are also delicious with a dribble of Green Harissa (see page 15) or Tzatziki (see page 67).

SERVES 4 AS A STARTER

Cheese-stuffed Kataifi

STUFFING

1 tablespoon olive oil

2 small shallots, finely chopped

1 clove garlic, finely chopped

100 g (3½ oz) grated haloumi

100 g (3½ oz) chopped
Fiore di Latte

120 g (4 oz) chopped fetta

100 g (3½ oz) pine nuts, fried
until golden brown

30 g (1 oz) breadcrumbs

1 egg

1 egg yolk

1 tablespoon roughly chopped
coriander (cilantro) leaves

1 tablespoon roughly
chopped parsley leaves

1 tablespoon roughly
chopped mint leaves

zest of ½ lemon

3 dried figs, diced and soaked in
water for 30 minutes

180 g (6 oz) kataifi pastry

180 g (6 oz) unsalted
butter, melted

freshly ground white pepper

1 tablespoon Za'atar (see page 4)

These crunchy, cheesy pastries are definitely not for the calorie-conscious, as they need liberal brushing with butter to make them crisp and golden. Kataifi is a noodle-like wheat pastry, probably best known in sweet pastries, but it works just as well for savouries. The tiny pieces of fig add a nice sweetness to the richness of the cheese. If you can't find Fiore di Latte, any other mozzarella will do.

This quantity makes 8 good-sized pastries to eat as a starter, and they also work well baby-size, as canapés for a drinks party.

To make the stuffing, heat the olive oil in a frying pan and sauté the shallots and garlic for a few minutes, until they soften. Allow to cool.

In a large mixing bowl combine the cheeses with the pine nuts, breadcrumbs, egg and egg yolk. Add the shallots mixture, all the herbs and lemon zest. Drain the excess liquid from the figs, add them to the cheese mixture and mix everything well. Use your hands to form the cheese into 8 neat golfballs and keep to one side.

Carefully unfold the kataifi pastry into 1 long skein and ease away half. Return the rest to the packet, seal tightly and refrigerate or freeze for future use. Trim the pastry to 25 cm (10 in) long pieces and carefully divide into 8 sections. Work with one section at a time, keeping the rest covered with a damp tea-towel to prevent it drying out. Bunch the strands together tightly, and lay out in a strip along the work surface. Brush along the length of the pastry with melted butter and sprinkle with white pepper. Place a golfball of cheese at one end and roll it up halfway along the pastry. Then carefully turn the parcel about 180 degrees and roll the remaining pastry across the other way. You should end up with a fat criss-crossed pastry ball. Repeat with the remaining pastry and cheese. Cover the pastries with a damp cloth and refrigerate for at least 30 minutes before baking.

Preheat the oven to 180°C (350°F).

Place the pastries on a baking tray lined with baking paper and cook them in the centre of the oven for 8–10 minutes, until they are golden brown and crisp. Drain on kitchen paper and serve immediately, sprinkled with Za'atar.

SERVES 4 AS A STARTER

Spanokopita Turbans

50 ml (1½ fl oz) olive oil

2 shallots, finely sliced

1 clove garlic, finely chopped

2 large bunches spinach, stalks removed and leaves shredded

150 g (5 oz) fetta

¼ teaspoon grated nutmeg

1 teaspoon dried mint

salt and pepper

8 sheets prepared filo pastry

100 g (3½ oz) butter, melted

These mini versions of the famous Greek spinach pie look really cute as a starter or a snack, and can also serve as an accompaniment to a garlicky roast lamb or barbecued porterhouse steak. Spinach and cheese are a marriage made in heaven, and the nutmeg and mint add a lovely fragrance to the filling.

Heat the olive oil in a heavy-based large pot. Add the shallots and garlic and stir over a medium heat for a few minutes until they soften. Now turn the heat right up and add the spinach. Stir around for a minute or so until the spinach collapses down, then tip everything out into a sieve and sit it over the sink to let the liquid drain away. Press on it firmly to help the process along a bit. When you've extracted as much moisture as you can, put the spinach mixture into the fridge to chill.

Preheat the oven to 200°C (400°F).

Take the spinach mixture out of the fridge and crumble in the fetta. Add the nutmeg and mint and season with a little salt and pepper.

Lay a sheet of filo pastry out on the work surface and brush lightly with melted butter. Arrange a long thin sausage of spinach filling along one length of the pastry, then roll up fairly loosely. Brush with a little more butter, then start to coil the pastry into a turban shape. Start at the base, and coil inwards and upwards, about two-and-a-half to three circles high. Tuck in the top so it looks neat. Continue with the remaining pastry and filling. You should have enough to make 8 little turbans.

Place all the little turbans onto a lightly greased baking sheet, brush with melted butter, and cook for 8–10 minutes or until they are golden brown.

SERVES 4

French Onion Pizza
with Turkish Sausage

DOUGH

1 x 8 g ($^1/_3$ oz) sachet dried yeast

250 ml (8 fl oz) warm water

2 tablespoons milk

2 tablespoons olive oil

300 g (10 oz) strong white flour

1 tablespoon salt

extra olive oil

TOPPING

60 ml (2 fl oz) olive oil

4 purple onions, finely sliced

1 tablespoon currants

1 tablespoon fresh thyme leaves

zest of $^1/_2$ lemon

200 g (7 oz) Turkish sausage, very finely sliced

100 g ($3^1/_2$ oz) mozzarella, grated

60 g (2 oz) black olives, pitted

4 eggs (optional)

Who can resist pizza? Popular in so many different cultures, it supports endless variations and interpretations. This is one of our favourites, with a lovely crisp base and topped with a soft oniony stew. The currants and spicy Turkish sausage turn it into something rather exotic, and if you want to make it into even more of a meal, then try cracking eggs on top before popping it into the oven.

To make the pizza dough, in a warm bowl, mix the yeast with half the warm water and stir well until completely dissolved. Next, add a heaped tablespoon of the flour and mix well to combine. Leave the mixture in a warm place for about 20 minutes until it forms a spongy mass.

Put the remaining flour into the mixing bowl of an electric mixer fitted with a dough hook. Add the milk, olive oil, salt and the yeast mixture. Knead for 10–15 minutes, adding a little more warm water if necessary, to make a silky smooth and rather wet dough. Smooth a little extra olive oil over the dough, cover with a cloth, and leave in a warm place to rise for 1–2 hours. The long rising time is what makes the pizza base crisp and crunchy.

Knock the dough back and knead a few times. Rub with a little more olive oil and put back into the bowl, covered, for another 30 minutes.

Meanwhile, preheat the oven and a 30 cm x 40 cm (12 in x 16 in) baking sheet to 220°C (425°F).

To make the filling, heat the oil in a frying pan and sauté the onions and currants for about 10 minutes to make a nice, soft stew. Towards the end of the time, add the thyme and lemon zest.

When the dough is ready, roll it out on a lightly floured surface into the shape of your baking sheet. Spread with the onion mixture and lay slices of sausage on top. Sprinkle over the mozzarella and olives and crack on the eggs, if using. Bake for 8–10 minutes or until the pastry is a nice golden-brown. Cut into portions and serve immediately.

SERVES 4

Spanish Omelette with Potato, Green Olives and Chorizo

100 ml (3½ fl oz) olive oil

1 onion, roughly chopped

3 potatoes, sliced

2 cloves garlic, roughly chopped

180 g (6 oz) semi-dried chorizo sausage, thickly sliced

a handful of large green olives, pitted

1 tablespoon chopped parsley leaves

8 large eggs

15 strands saffron, lightly roasted and crushed

salt and pepper

This is the kind of dish that we love to knock up as an impromptu supper dish, using up whatever leftovers we can find. This omelette is closer to an Italian frittata – thick and chunky, rather than semi-soft and folded like the French version. In Spain they'd be just as likely to colour the eggs with saffron to make a deep rich golden tortilla. We include it in the ingredients here, but feel free to vary the recipe as you choose. The real beauty of a meal like this is that you can throw in whatever goodies you can find in the fridge.

Our version, true to its Spanish roots, includes potatoes, thick chunks of spicy chorizo and the salty tang of large green olives. If you have any red peppers around, or tomatoes, throw them in for extra colour. This omelette is lovely eaten warm for supper or lunch, and is also delicious eaten cold. Cut it into wedges and include it in a mezze selection, or take it on a picnic. You might even try it out in the kids' school lunch box.

Heat half the olive oil in a heavy-based frying pan. Use one that is fairly deep and not too large, or you'll end with a flat pancake affair, rather than a dense deep eggy cake. Sauté the onion and potatoes on a medium heat for 10–15 minutes until they soften. You will need to stir them fairly often to make sure that they remain uncoloured. Add the garlic, chorizo, olives and parsley and mix everything together. Cook for a few more minutes over a medium heat, then transfer to a bowl.

Lightly whisk the eggs with the saffron and season with salt and pepper. Wipe out the pan, then pour in the remaining olive oil and heat. Pour the eggs over the potato mixture, then tip everything into the pan. Cook on a high heat for a couple of minutes, until it starts to set on the underside, and bubble and puff up around the edges. Lower the heat, cover the pan and cook for about 8 minutes or so, or until the eggs set.

Take the pan to the table, cut the omelette into wedges and serve with a green leaf salad.

SERVES 4

Lebanese Club Sandwich with Crab, Avocado and Tabbouleh

8 mini pitta ('jou-jou') breads

100 ml (3½ fl oz) Taramasalata (see page 63)

2 Lebanese cucumbers, thinly sliced

200 g (7 oz) fresh crabmeat

1 avocado, peeled, stoned and finely sliced

salt and pepper

lemon juice

TABBOULEH

½ cup parsley leaves

1 tablespoon finely chopped mint leaves

1 tomato, finely chopped

1 shallot, finely chopped

1 tablespoon burghul wheat, soaked in water for 10 minutes

a pinch of allspice

a pinch of ground cinnamon

salt and pepper

olive oil

lemon juice

With its pretty pastel shades and light, lemony flavours, this makes a terrific summer starter, or a posh lunch sandwich. As with all club sandwiches, it's really about the combination of textures and flavours. Here you get the scent of the sea from the crab and taramasalata, some spice and herbs from the tabbouleh, and crunchy freshness from the cucumber. The mini pitta breads really must be very fresh, but as they freeze well, the best thing to do is buy them when you see them and store them in the freezer until ready to use.

To make the tabbouleh, put the parsley, mint, tomato and shallots into a mixing bowl. Squeeze the cracked wheat dry of as much water as you can. Add it to the mixing bowl and then add the spices, salt and pepper, olive oil and lemon juice. Mix well, then taste and adjust the seasoning if necessary.

For each sandwich, you will need 2 mini pitta breads. Split them in half, spread one piece with taramasalata and layer with cucumber. Spoon on a tablespoon of crabmeat and cover with another piece of bread. Now layer with avocado, sprinkle with salt and pepper, squeeze on a little lemon juice and then dollop on a spoonful of tabbouleh. Cover with another layer of bread. For the final third, spread again with a thin layer of taramasalata, layer with cucumber and then pile on the remaining crabmeat. Top with the final piece of bread.

Repeat for the remaining three sandwiches. Use a very sharp knife to cut each sandwich in half and serve with potato crisps!

SERVES 4

Taramasalata

100 g (3½ oz) tarama
2 thick-cut slices good quality
white bread
1 clove garlic, roughly chopped
juice of 1–1½ lemons
250 ml (8 fl oz) olive oil
250 ml (8 fl oz) vegetable oil
about 100 ml (3½ fl oz) water

It might seem strange to include a recipe for taramasalata, given that it is available just about everywhere these days. But sadly, the plastic tubs of lurid pink gloop sold as taramasalata bear scant resemble to the original version. In its true form, it is a creamy smooth, pinky golden purée, tangy with garlic and lemon juice, and bursting with flavours of the sea. And it couldn't be easier to make, requiring nothing more than a little blitzing in a food processor. When you've tasted the light, fluffy and far subtler homemade version, you'll never buy it ready-made again!

Tarama itself is the salted preserved roe of grey mullet (commercial versions are often made from the less expensive cod's roe) and comes as a very firm, hot-pink paste. Avoid any that seems to have an orange tinge, as it is likely to be bitter.

Lightly rinse the tarama under cold running water for about 30 seconds to rinse away some of the excess salt.

Slice away the crusts from the bread and chop the bread roughly. Put it into a mixing bowl and pour on enough water to cover. Then fish out the bread and squeeze it tightly. Put the scrunched-up bread into the food processor with the tarama, garlic and the juice of one of the lemons and whiz everything to a paste.

Mix the two oils together and start to drizzle them into the processor. Begin with about 100 ml (3½ fl oz) of oil, then loosen the mixture up with about 2 tablespoons water. Continue adding first the oil, then the water in similar quantities, and finish with the remaining lemon juice. The purée should be light and fluffy and the prettiest pale pink golden colour.

Taste the taramasalata and adjust the balance if necessary. Tip it into a container, cover and refrigerate where it will keep for 4–5 days.

MAKES ABOUT 500 G (1 LB)

Green Split Pea Dip with Black Olives and Goat's Cheese

1 onion, finely diced

2 tablespoons olive oil

2 cloves garlic, finely chopped

200 g (7 oz) green split peas, soaked overnight

300 ml (10 fl oz) water

$1/3$ whole nutmeg, grated

salt and pepper

2 tablespoons extra virgin olive oil

80 g ($2^1/_2$ oz) goat's cheese, roughly crumbled

10 large black olives, pitted and roughly chopped

The sweet starchiness of split peas makes them the ideal base for purées and dips. The bright green colour is really very pretty, and the little creamy nuggets of goat's cheese and salty chips of black olive make a lovely surprise. Scoop it up with plenty of fresh Arabic bread.

In a large saucepan, sauté the onion in the olive oil until it is soft and transparent, taking care not to let it colour. Add the garlic and sauté for a few more minutes. Now, pour in the split peas and enough of the water to cover the peas by two finger-widths.

Bring to the boil, then lower the heat and allow to simmer gently for 30–40 minutes, until the peas have broken down to a green mush and the water has nearly all evaporated. Season the mixture with the nutmeg, salt and pepper, and allow to cool slightly. Whisk the extra virgin olive oil into the mix, and fold through the goat's cheese and olives. Check the seasoning and allow to cool completely.

MAKES ABOUT 300 G (10 OZ)

Front: (L) Mint Labne (recipe page 67); (R) Taramasalata (recipe page 63);
Middle: Green Split Pea Dip (recipe this page); Top: Tzatziki (recipe page 67)

Hummus bi Tahini

250 g (8 oz) chickpeas

2 tablespoons bicarbonate of
soda (baking soda)

juice of up to 2 lemons

2 small cloves garlic, crushed
with 1 teaspoon sea salt

100 ml (3½ fl oz) tahini
paste, well stirred

salt and pepper

One of the very best things about food and cooking is that there are always new and improved ways of doing things. This recipe for hummus is a case in point. Greg learnt this method while helping his brother and sister-in-law and their friend Dodo Talj set up the kitchen at their new eatery, Cafe Zum Zum in North Carlton. During this cooking stint he had the pleasure of working with Bassouma, a Lebanese cook who has worked at some of the best Middle Eastern restaurants around Melbourne. Her hummus is legendary!

This version uses a lot of bicarbonate of soda in the soaking process, which helps break the pulses down. They are then cooked down to a mush and blitzed, skins and all. The result is a superlative, super-smooth dip, rather than the usual, rather gritty version.

Soak the chickpeas overnight in twice their volume of cold water and the bicarbonate of soda. The next day, rinse the chickpeas very thoroughly. Don't rush this step – you should take at least 5–10 minutes rinsing them under cold running water. Place them in a large pan of fresh water and bring to the boil. Then lower the heat and simmer for up to 2 hours, until they have disintegrated to a porridge-like mush. You will need to keep an eye on them during the cooking process, and top up with extra water every 20 minutes or so.

Tip the chickpeas into a processor with the lemon juice, garlic paste and tahini and whiz until the mixture is very smooth. Taste and adjust the seasoning until you get the right balance of nuttiness, acid and pungent garlic.

As it cools, the hummus will thicken, so thin it down with a little more lemon juice or water as needed.

MAKES ABOUT 500 G (1 LB)

Tzatziki

1 kg (2 lb) natural yoghurt, strained overnight or for 24 hours

2 Lebanese cucumbers, seeded and grated (skin on)

1 clove garlic, crushed with 1 teaspoon sea salt

1 teaspoon dried mint

½ cup roughly chopped mint leaves

juice of 1 lemon

salt and pepper

A terrific cooling dip that goes with so many things. Homemade tzatziki is simple to make, and infinitely superior to any shop-bought version – the flavours are much richer and more vibrant.

Mix all the ingredients together in a large bowl and season with a little salt and pepper. Chill until required.

MAKES ABOUT 600 G (20 OZ)

Mint Labne

1 kg (2 lb) plain yoghurt

200 g (7 oz) extra yoghurt

½ cup mint leaves

½ cup parsley leaves

1 teaspoon dried mint

1 teaspoon salt

Labne (yoghurt cheese) is the simplest of cheeses made regularly around the Middle East. It is infinitely versatile and lends itself to savoury and sweet flavourings. You could try adding a teaspoon of garlic purée, for instance, or swirl in a spoonful of harissa, or other fresh herb purées such as basil, oregano or dill. Sweet versions can be made with a splash of rosewater, orange-blossom water or a fragrant honey.

Spoon the kilo of yoghurt into a clean muslin square, cheesecloth or tea-towel. Tie the four corners together and suspend the bundle from a wooden spoon over a deep bowl. Put it in the refrigerator and allow it to drain overnight.

The next day, tip the extra yoghurt into a blender and put the mint and parsley leaves on top. Blitz until it's a nice fine, pale green purée. Put the labne into a mixing bowl with the dried mint and salt. Stir together well, then swirl in the green purée for a pretty marbled effect. Serve as an accompaniment to spicy soups and braises, grilled poultry and meats, and traditional Middle Eastern favourites such as stuffed vine leaves and cabbage rolls.

MAKES ABOUT 500 G (1 LB)

Smoked Eel Brandade with Paprika and Toasted Arabic Bread

1 large smoked eel, about 500 g (1 lb) whole weight

2 medium-sized floury potatoes, peeled

300 ml (10 fl oz) milk

250 ml (8 fl oz) water

3 cloves garlic, cut in half

1 tablespoon extra virgin olive oil

zest of ½ lemon

½ onion, studded with 2 cloves

1 bay leaf

2 long green mild chillies, split in half, seeded and scraped

1 tablespoon red wine vinegar

TO SERVE

80 ml (1½ fl oz) extra virgin olive oil

1 tablespoon red wine vinegar

1 teaspoon sweet paprika

2 shallots, very finely chopped

freshly ground black pepper

Arabic bread

Brandade is the classic Portuguese pâté made from saltcod and potato. Here we use smoked eel, which is rich, oily and has an intense smoky flavour that blends well with the bland smoothness of mashed potato. To serve, add a splash of good quality red wine vinegar to cut through its richness. It works well as a dip or as part of a mezze selection.

Prepare the eel by chopping off its head and cutting the body into 5–6 chunks through the central bone. Cut the potatoes into large chunks. Put the eel and potatoes into a largish saucepan with the milk, water, garlic, olive oil, lemon zest, onion, bay leaf and chillies. Bring to the boil, then lower the heat and simmer for about 15 minutes, or until the potatoes are well cooked.

Remove the pan from the heat and discard the onion, lemon zest, bay leaf and chillies. Tip the rest of the ingredients through a sieve, reserving the milk for later. When cool enough to handle, put the eel into a mixing bowl, peel away the skin and pull the flesh off the bones. Discard the skin and bones. Use a fork to shred the flesh roughly.

Roughly mash the potatoes and garlic with about 50 ml (1½ fl oz) of the poaching liquid and the vinegar, then mix in the shredded eel. What you are aiming for is a coarsely textured kind of pâté. Add a little more milk if necessary, bearing in mind that the mixture will thicken as it chills. Tip into a container and refrigerate overnight.

When you are ready to serve, whisk together the extra virgin olive oil, vinegar, paprika, shallots and pepper to make a dressing. Scoop a mound of the brandade onto each serving plate and make an indentation with the back of a hot soup spoon. Carefully pour in a little of the dressing and serve with plenty of toasted Arabic bread.

SERVES 6 AS A STARTER

grains, pasta & pulses

Preserved Lemon Risotto

60 ml (2 fl oz) olive oil

1 small onion, quartered

400 g (14 oz) Vialone Nano rice

60 ml (2 fl oz) white wine

up to 1 litre (2 pints) chicken or vegetable stock, simmering

1 Preserved Lemon (see pages 20–1), skin only, finely diced

1 tablespoon chopped celery leaves (from the heart)

100 g (3½ oz) unsalted butter, chilled and diced

60 g (2 oz) parmesan, grated

salt and pepper

A lovely refreshing risotto with a salty lemon tang. It makes a nice accompaniment to a rich braise such as oxtail, or use it as a garnish with Mussel Mulligatawny Soup (see page 33).

Heat the oil in a pan and add the onion. Fry for a few minutes to flavour the oil, then discard. Add the rice and stir for a few minutes to coat each grain of rice with the oil. Add the wine and let it bubble away until evaporated. Next, ladle in enough simmering stock to cover the rice by a finger's width. Cook on medium heat, stirring with a wooden spoon from time to time, until most of the stock has been absorbed.

Add the same quantity of stock. Again, cook on medium heat, stirring from time to time, until most of the stock has been absorbed.

Add a third amount of stock (reserve around 100 ml/3½ fl oz for the final stage) and when half of the liquid has been absorbed, add the preserved lemon and celery and stir gently until the stock is all absorbed.

Stir in the butter and parmesan and season with salt and pepper. Add the final 100 ml (3½ fl oz) of stock and stir until the butter and cheese have melted. Cover the pot and allow to rest away from the heat for a few minutes. Taste and adjust the seasoning if needed, and serve straight away.

SERVES 4 AS A STARTER OR LIGHT LUNCH DISH

Eggplant Rice Pilaf
with Hilbeh and Yoghurt

EGGPLANT PILAF

2 medium-sized eggplant
(aubergine)

salt

400 g (14 oz) long-grain rice

100 ml (3½ fl oz) olive oil

1 onion, finely chopped

1 clove garlic, finely chopped

1 x 400 g (14 oz) can
chopped tomatoes

salt and freshly ground
black pepper

1 tablespoon roughly
chopped mint

1 tablespoon roughly
chopped parsley

500 ml (16 fl oz) stock
or water, boiling

TO SERVE

100 ml (3½ fl oz) Hilbeh
(see page 17)

100 ml (3½ fl oz) plain yoghurt

Arabic bread

A lovely thick and sticky rice dish, full of satiny chunks of eggplant in a rich tomatoey base, while the mint adds a nice refreshing balance. Serve the hilbeh on the side as a spicy relish, and add a blob of creamy smooth yoghurt to smooth it all out in the mouth.

Cut the eggplant into 1 cm (⅓ in) dice, put them into a colander and sprinkle lightly with salt. This draws out some of the moisture and reduces the amount of oil absorbed during the cooking. Leave for 20 minutes while you prepare the remaining ingredients.

Put the rice into a bowl and wash under cold running water until it runs clear – you want to wash away as much of the excess starch as possible.

Heat two-thirds of the oil in a heavy-based pan and gently sauté the eggplant until they are lightly coloured. Remove them from the pan with a slotted spoon and set aside. Add the rest of the oil to the pan, then the onion and garlic, and fry gently until they soften. Return the eggplant to the pan and tip in the tomatoes. Season with salt and pepper, then throw in the mint and parsley and mix well.

Add the rice to the pan – you don't want to mix it in, but rather layer it on top of the vegetable stew. This stops the eggplant breaking down into the rice. Carefully pour on the boiling water or stock. Return it to the boil without stirring, cover the pan, reduce the heat and simmer for 25 minutes.

When the cooking time is up, turn off the heat and remove the lid. Cover the pan with a tea-towel, replace the lid and leave to stand for 10 minutes to steam. To serve, gently mix the rice and the braised vegetables together, and serve with the accompaniments of hilbeh and yoghurt and plenty of Arabic bread.

SERVES 6–8

Golden Saffron Pumpkin Risotto with Watercress Salad

RISOTTO

60 ml (2 fl oz) olive oil

1 small onion, quartered

400 g (14 oz) Vialone Nano rice

60 ml (2 fl oz) white wine

up to 1 litre (2 pints) chicken or
vegetable stock, simmering

200 g (7 oz) butternut pumpkin,
cut into small (1 cm/$^1/_3$ in) dice

15 strands saffron, lightly toasted
and crushed

1 tablespoon chopped parsley

1 tablespoon chopped celery
leaves (from the heart)

100 g (3$^1/_2$ oz) unsalted butter,
chilled and cut into small cubes

60 g (2 oz) parmesan, grated

salt and pepper

WATERCRESS SALAD

juice of $^1/_2$ lemon

2 tablespoons extra virgin
olive oil

salt and pepper

1 bunch watercress,
large stalks removed (about
$^3/_4$ cup leaves)

1 cup baby curly endive

$^1/_2$ purple onion,
very finely sliced

**There is something irresistibly gentle and soothing about a bowl of creamy risotto.
Here, the sweet starchiness of pumpkin and mysterious bittersweet pungency of
saffron transform the rice into a glorious, golden hued meal.**

Heat the oil in a pan and add the onion. Fry for a few minutes to flavour the oil, then
discard. Add the rice and stir for a few minutes to coat each grain of rice with the oil.
Add the wine and let it bubble away until evaporated. Next, ladle in enough simmering
stock to cover the rice by a finger's width. Cook on medium heat, stirring with a wooden
spoon from time to time, until most of the stock has been absorbed.

Add the same quantity of stock. Again, cook on medium heat, stirring from time
to time, until most of the stock has been absorbed.

Add a third amount of stock (reserve around 100 ml/3$^1/_2$ fl oz for the final stage)
and when half of the liquid has been absorbed, add the pumpkin, saffron, parsley
and celery. Stir gently until the stock is all absorbed.

Stir in the butter and parmesan and season with salt and pepper. Add the final
100 ml (3$^1/_2$ fl oz) of stock and stir until the butter and cheese have melted. Cover the
pot and allow to rest off the heat for a few minutes. Taste and adjust the seasoning.

To make the watercress salad, whisk together the lemon juice, oil, salt and pepper
and dress the watercress leaves, endive and onion.

Serve the risotto immediately, topped with a small mound of salad.

SERVES 4

Rabbit Paella with Chorizo and Hungarian Peppers

4 mild green Hungarian peppers

500 g (1 lb) arroz de Valencia

2 tablespoons olive oil

1.4 kg (2¾ lb) rabbit, jointed

2 onions, finely sliced

2 cloves garlic, finely sliced

150 g (5 oz) chorizo sausage, sliced fairly thickly

1 x 400 g (14 oz) can tomatoes

6 preserved artichokes, halved

100 g (3½ oz) fresh peas*

1 bullet chilli, seeded, scraped and finely chopped

12 strands saffron, roasted in a dry pan and crushed

1 tablespoon sweet paprika

200 ml (7 fl oz) white wine

1.2 litres (2½ pints) chicken or vegetable stock, simmering

salt and pepper

* If using frozen peas, add them with the second quantity of stock.

Paella, Spain's most famous dish, is a satisfying peasant meal combining rice, meat and fish and flavoured with saffron. Its varieties are myriad – fancy tourist versions usually include an abundance of seafood, chicken and rabbit; simpler versions are mainly beans and vegetables with a little meat for flavour. The true original, however, coming as it did from the wetlands of Valencia, uses eel, snails and green beans.

To the paella purist, the bits that go into the dish are almost incidental. It is the rice that is the key to a successful paella, and the locally grown product, arroz de Valencia, is essential. Paella is traditionally cooked by men on an outdoor barbecue using a shallow wide-bottomed pan that helps produce the very desirable crust underneath the rice. The finished dish should be dry rather than wet and soupy.

Making paella is fairly hard work – certainly in the preparation – so it's worth doing in fairly large quantities for a special occasion. As not many of us have a proper paella pan at home, you will probably achieve the best result using a heavy-based wide baking dish.

Preheat the oven to 200°C (400°F). Place the peppers on a baking tray and roast until the skins start to blister and blacken, turning from time to time. Remove them from the oven and tip into a bowl. Cover with cling film and leave to steam for a further 10 minutes, which softens the peppers and loosens the skin. Carefully peel the peppers, discarding the skin, stalks and seeds. Slice the flesh lengthways.

Put the rice into a bowl and wash under cold running water until it runs clear. Set aside until ready to use.

Heat the olive oil in a large baking dish and add the rabbit, onions and garlic. Cook over a medium flame until they colour lightly and evenly. Add the chorizo and stir. Next, add the tomatoes, artichokes, peas, chilli, saffron and paprika and stir well. Add the rice, then the wine and half of the stock and stir in with the other ingredients. Lower the heat and cook until all the stock is absorbed. Then add the remaining stock (and frozen peas if using), and cook until the rice is tender. Do not stir, as this helps form the desirable crust at the bottom of the pan. Season to taste with salt and pepper, and bring the cooking pan to the table to serve.

SERVES 8

Lentils and Rice with Caramelised Onions

LENTILS
150 g (5 oz) brown lentils

½ onion

1 bay leaf

1 cinnamon stick

1 tablespoon extra virgin olive oil

CARAMELISED ONIONS
50 ml (1½ fl oz) olive oil

a knob of unsalted butter

3 medium-sized purple onions, finely sliced

RISOTTO
2 tablespoons olive oil

½ small onion, finely diced

200 g (7 oz) Vialone Nano rice

60 ml (2 fl oz) white wine

up to 1 litre (2 pints) chicken or vegetable stock, simmering

80 g (2½ oz) unsalted butter, chilled and diced

40 g (1¼ oz) parmesan, grated

salt and pepper

In the Middle East, as in other parts of the world, lentils are often combined with rice to add an easy protein boost. This dish is similar to mjaddarah, one of the most popular home-cooked dishes in Lebanon and Syria. In mjaddarah, the rice and lentils are cooked together until they break down to a sludge-coloured kind of porridge. Here, the rice is prepared risotto-style, and the cooked lentils are added towards the end for a pretty speckled effect. Serve with the caramelised onions spooned lavishly over the top, and a chunky salad, such as the Greek Rocket Salad on page 39.

To cook the lentils, put them in a pan with twice their volume of water, the onion, bay leaf and cinnamon stick. Bring to the boil, then lower the heat and cook for 25–30 minutes, or until the lentils are tender. Remove the pan from the heat, drain off the water, discard the aromatics and stir through the olive oil.

Prepare the caramelised onions while you are making the risotto. Heat the oil and butter in a heavy-based frying pan and cook the onions over a very slow heat for 10–15 minutes until they are soft and sweet.

To cook the risotto, heat the oil and fry the onion for a few minutes to flavour the oil, then discard. Add the rice and stir for a few minutes to coat each grain of rice with the oil. Pour in the wine and let it bubble away until it evaporates. Next, ladle in enough simmering stock to cover the rice by a finger's width. Cook on medium heat, stirring with a wooden spoon from time to time, until most of the stock has been absorbed.

Add the same quantity of stock. Again, cook on medium heat, stirring from time to time, until most of the stock has been absorbed.

Add a third amount of stock (reserve around 100 ml/3½ fl oz for the final stage) and when half of the liquid has been absorbed, add the lentils. Stir gently until the stock is all absorbed.

Stir in the butter and parmesan and season with salt and pepper. Add the final 100 ml (3½ fl oz) of stock and stir until the butter and cheese have melted. Cover and allow to rest off the heat for a few minutes. Taste and adjust the seasoning.

Serve in shallow bowls, topped with a generous spoonful of caramelised onions.

SERVES 4

Fried Parmesan Polenta
with Tomato Harissa

2 litres (4 pints) water

½ teaspoon salt

300 g (10 oz) polenta

75 g (2½ oz) parmesan, grated

2 tablespoons unsalted butter

salt and pepper

plain flour for dusting

100 ml (3½ fl oz) vegetable
oil for shallow-frying

TOMATO HARISSA

1 tablespoon Red Harissa
(see page 16)

1 tablespoon extra virgin
olive oil

1 x 400 g (14 oz) can
chopped tomatoes

salt and pepper

Fiery harissa is one of those condiments that go well with so many things. As is so often the case with chilli-based foods, it has a strangely addictive quality, and you will probably end up wanting more and more of it! Here, its peppery heat is the perfect counterpoint to the rich buttery smoothness of polenta. We also like to add parmesan for a cheesy tang, and then to cut the thickened, cold polenta into chip-like wedges and fry them to a crunchy crispness. Provide a bowl of harissa as a little dipping sauce and serve the polenta with a mixed-leaf salad.

Pour the water into a large heavy-based pan (we use a Le Creuset, which is ideal) and bring to the boil. Add the salt, and with the water bubbling away, pour in the polenta in a fine, steady stream, stirring very well with a stiff whisk until it all incorporates into a wet grainy mass. Now turn the heat down low to cook. The polenta will take 20–30 minutes of cooking and steady stirring, which, we must admit, requires both strong muscles and determination. What you want to end up with is a completely smooth yellow mass that comes away from the sides of the pan in a smooth ball. It is a little tedious, but the polenta needs all that time to lose its graininess and you can console yourself with the knowledge that you end up with an infinitely superior result than you will ever get from the instant variety.

When the polenta is cooked, remove the pan from the heat and stir in the cheese and butter. Taste it for seasoning and add more salt if necessary, and pepper to taste.

Pour the polenta into a 30 x 24 cm (12 x 9½ in) baking dish lined with greaseproof paper, smooth the surface with a wet spatula and leave it to set. When completely cold, tip out onto a work surface, peel off the greaseproof paper and cut the polenta into any shape you like (small diamonds, thick-cut wedges and so on). Lightly dust with the flour before frying.

To make the tomato harissa, blend together the harissa paste, olive oil and the tomatoes to make a thick sauce. Season to taste with salt and pepper.

We like to serve this polenta cut into thick chips as an accompaniment to a hearty braise or stew. You can either deep-fry or shallow-fry them until they turn a lovely golden colour. Serve with the tomato harissa on the side as a dipping sauce.

SERVES 8

Couscous Stew with Grilled Calamari and Zhoug

COUSCOUS

60 ml (2 fl oz) olive oil

1 medium-sized onion, finely chopped

2 cloves garlic, crushed with 1 teaspoon sea salt

1 tablespoon coriander seeds, roasted and ground

1 tablespoon cumin seeds, roasted and ground

1 teaspoon allspice

1 teaspoon chilli powder

1 teaspoon sweet paprika

1 x 400 g (14 oz) can chopped tomatoes

1 green chilli, seeded, scraped and finely shredded

1 teaspoon honey

salt and pepper

100 g ($3^1/_2$ oz) couscous

100 g ($3^1/_2$ oz) chickpeas, soaked and cooked

1 tablespoon finely chopped parsley

1 tablespoon finely chopped mint

12 medium-sized squid tubes, split and scored on the outside

80 ml ($2^1/_2$ fl oz) olive oil

$^1/_2$ cup Zhoug (see page 17)

juice of 1 lemon

There is nothing quite like the aroma of calamari on the grill to awaken memories of holidays by the sea. So fire up the barbecue and eat this in the garden on a hot summer's night. The couscous is thick, rich and intensely spicy – the perfect foil to simply grilled calamari. It is also delicious served cold. Zhoug is a fiercely hot coriander relish, which is the perfect condiment for many seafood dishes.

To make the couscous, heat the olive oil in a heavy-based saucepan, add the onion and cook over a gentle heat until soft. Then add the garlic, coriander, cumin, allspice, chilli powder and paprika, and mix well. Cook for a further 2 minutes, then add the tomatoes, green chilli and honey. Cook for another 10 minutes, then taste for seasoning.

Now add the couscous and chickpeas, cover the pan and cook over a low heat until the couscous swells and softens. This will take 5–10 minutes.

When you are ready to eat, heat the grill (broiler) or barbecue to its highest temperature. Brush the squid with olive oil and season, then place the squid, scored side down, on the hot plate. After 40 seconds, turn them over. In a few moments, they will curl into a tight cylinder. Cook for no more than a minute, then remove from the heat.

To serve, stir the parsley and mint through the couscous. Place the calamari on top and dot with tiny blobs of zhoug (be careful, it is very hot!). Sprinkle with lemon juice, and serve with plenty of warm Arabic bread.

SERVES 6

Wild Mushroom Couscous with Fiore di Latte

2 tablespoons extra virgin olive oil

250 ml (8 fl oz) water

500 g (1 lb) couscous

½ teaspoon salt

100 g (3½ oz) dried porcini mushrooms

2 ripe tomatoes, skinned, seeded and diced

150 g (5 oz) Fiore di Latte (or mozzarella)

1 tablespoon extra virgin olive oil

a dusting of sweet paprika

Wild mushrooms such as porcini (or cèpes) have an intensely dark earthiness about them. Steaming the couscous with the soaking liquor, as we do here, impregnates the couscous with the very essence of mushroom.

Sprinkle the oil and water onto the couscous and rub it between your fingers for a few minutes until all the grains are coated. Leave it to sit for 20 minutes so the grains start to absorb the moisture and swell. Then take a fork and work through the couscous to break down any lumps.

Soak the mushrooms in twice their volume of cold water for about 10 minutes.

Tip the couscous into a steamer lined with a tea-towel, and seal around the sides with cling film. Steam for 20–30 minutes over rapidly boiling water, uncovered, until the couscous grains soften and become fluffy. Remove from the heat and tip into a heatproof serving bowl. Gently rub the grains between your fingers until they run smoothly, then season with salt.

Strain the soaking liquid from the mushrooms and pour it into the bottom of the steamer. Return the couscous to the steamer, add the mushrooms and tomatoes, and steam for a further 20 minutes.

Turn the grill (broiler) to its highest temperature. Grate the cheese over the couscous, sprinkle with olive oil and pop the dish under the grill until the cheese melts. Serve sprinkled with a little paprika.

SERVES 4

Giant Couscous

500 ml (16 fl oz) boiling water
200 g (7 oz) moghrabieh
1 tablespoon olive oil
a pinch of salt
a pinch of Ras al Hanout
(see page 3)

COOKING STOCK
1 litre (2 pints) water
1 onion
1 bullet chilli
1 cinnamon stick
10 strands saffron
1/2 teaspoon cardamom seeds
2 bay leaves

2 tablespoons extra virgin
olive oil
1/4 teaspoon Ras al Hanout
(see page 3)
salt

Couscous, the daily diet of North Africa, is hugely popular in Western countries these days. This giant couscous is the Lebanese version – they call it *moghrabieh* (from the Maghreb). The semolina grains are much larger than the Moroccan version we are familiar with, and during cooking they swell almost to the size of small peas.

Greg found this recipe in a book called the *Art of Lebanese Cooking* by George Rayess, which is the Lebanese housewife's bible! It has to be said that this is not a quick-cook dish. The moghrabieh need to be soaked first to remove some of the surface starch, then they are steamed or braised in a flavoursome broth for around 2 hours. But please don't let that put you off. The result is an incredibly pleasing mound of little pea-sized balls, fragrant from their cooking liquor, and soft and squishy in the mouth. In our view, they are worth the time they take to cook, not just for the novelty value, but because they work really well as a starchy accompaniment to all kinds of grilled meats, fish or poultry, as well as braises and casseroles.

Pour boiling water onto the moghrabieh, add the olive oil, salt and ras al hanout, and leave to stand for 10 minutes. Move the grains around from time to time so that they don't stick and clump together.

Fill the bottom of a steamer with 1 litre (2 pints) water, then add the aromatics. Put the moghrabieh into the top part of the steamer, cover and bring to the boil. Then lower the heat and steam for 2 hours over a medium flame. Check the water level every 30 minutes and top up with boiling water if necessary, and fork through the moghrabieh to keep it loose.

At the end of the 2 hours, check the consistency of the moghrabieh, which should have doubled in size. Each grain should be distinct and separate, not sticky, and they should be soft and tender.

Tip into a bowl and mix through the extra virgin olive oil, ras al hanout and salt to taste.

SERVES 4

Buttered Egg Noodles with Artichokes, Cèpes and Saffron

100 ml (3½ fl oz) extra virgin olive oil

2 purple onions, finely sliced

1 tablespoon Taklia (see page 9)

8–10 strands saffron, lightly toasted and crushed

8 preserved artichokes, halved

2 tomatoes, diced

100 g (3½ oz) fresh peas

½ Preserved Lemon (see pages 20–1), peel only, finely shredded

60 ml (2 fl oz) Vermouth or white wine

salt and freshly ground black pepper

50 g (1½ oz) dried cèpes, soaked in 200 ml (7 fl oz) cold water

juice of ½ lemon

400 g (14 oz) fresh Chinese egg noodles

a knob of unsalted butter

A delightfully simple supper dish of buttered egg noodles stirred through with artichokes, cèpes mushrooms (also known as porcini) and a savoury spice mix called taklia. Taklia is a kind of all-purpose mix found around the Middle East, which is commonly added at the end of cooking for an aromatic flavouring. It can also be thinned down with a little olive oil or enlivened with a touch of chilli and used as a condiment.

Heat the olive oil in a heavy-based pan, then add the onions and taklia and cook over a gentle heat until soft, about 5 minutes. Then add the saffron, artichokes, tomatoes, peas, preserved lemon and Vermouth and allow to bubble for a few minutes. Season with salt and pepper. Remove the cèpes from their soaking water and add them to the pan with a tablespoon of the liquid.

Cook the egg noodles in boiling water (they only take a minute or so), drain well and tip into a large serving bowl. Stir through the butter. Pour on the braised vegetables and mix in well. Serve straight away with warm crusty bread.

SERVES 4

Cracked Wheat Pilaf with Wild Mushrooms and Sour Cream

60 g (2 oz) dried porcini
mushrooms

300 g (10 oz) coarse-grade
burghul (cracked wheat)

1 litre (2 pints) cold water

salt and pepper

1/2 teaspoon allspice

zest of 1/2 orange

1 tablespoon unsalted butter

50 g (1 1/2 oz) toasted pine nuts

ground cinnamon

150 ml (5 fl oz) carton
sour cream

An intensely satisfying and wholesome supper dish – all earthy flavours and sweetly spiced overtones. Granted, in the Middle East they would probably be more inclined to use yoghurt as an accompaniment instead of sour cream. If you are conscious of your dairy intake then feel free to do the same.

Put the mushrooms in a bowl with 200 ml (7 fl oz) cold water and leave to soak for 10 minutes.

Meanwhile, rinse the burghul well in cold water and put in a pot with the cold water. Leave to soak for about 5 minutes.

Season the burghul with salt and pepper, then put on the heat and bring to the boil. Now turn down the heat, put the lid on the pan and let it simmer for 10 minutes. While the burghul is simmering, remove the mushrooms from their soaking water and chop them roughly.

When the 10 minutes are up, add the allspice, orange zest and the mushrooms to the burghul, fork them through to mix in well, cover the pan and allow to sit and steam in its own heat for a further 10 minutes.

When ready to serve, remove the lid, add the butter and fluff it through with a fork. Garnish with the pine nuts, dust with cinnamon and serve with a blob of sour cream.

SERVES 4

Crisp-fried Goat's Cheese Ravioli

2 shallots, finely chopped

1 clove garlic, finely chopped

1 tablespoon olive oil

150 g (5 oz) goat's cheese

$\frac{1}{2}$ teaspoon dried mint

salt and pepper

1 packet (about 150 g/5 oz) wonton wrappers

1 tablespoon cornflour (cornstarch) mixed with 1 tablespoon water

280 ml (9 fl oz) vegetable oil for deep-frying

A quick-and-easy kind of ravioli, which uses wonton skins or spring-roll wrappers rather than the more labour-intensive pasta dough. Dried mint is very popular in the Middle East and adds its own unique and quite delicious flavour to the tangy goat's cheese filling. The ravioli turn a beautiful golden-brown when fried, and are delicious slipped into a shallow bowl with a knob of butter or a drizzle of extra virgin olive oil and shavings of parmesan. Or, if you like, try them with any kind of sauce you might have in the fridge or pantry – a blob of garlicky salsa verde or pesto would be delicious. Salty tapenade or even a simple tomato sauce would also work very well.

Sauté the shallots and garlic in the olive oil for a few minutes until soft, then allow them to cool down.

Crumble the goat's cheese into a mixing bowl, then add the shallots mixture, mint, salt and pepper. Fork through well, but without breaking down the cheese too much.

Lay the wonton wrappers out on a work surface. Blob a teaspoon of the cheese onto each wrapper, then wet the edges with a little cornflour paste. Fold over diagonally and seal the edges to make little triangular ravioli. Continue until all the stuffing has been used.

Preheat the oven to 100°C (200°F) and put your serving dish in to warm.

Heat the vegetable oil in a medium-sized saucepan (or a deep-fryer) to 180°C (350°F), or until a cube of bread added to the oil sizzles to the top and turns golden brown in about 30 seconds.

Fry 6 ravioli at a time until they colour lightly. Remove from the oil and drain on kitchen paper. Keep them warm in the oven until all are cooked.

SERVES 4 AS A STARTER

French Lentils Sautéed with Bulgarian Fetta

200 g (7 oz) Puy lentils

1 medium-sized onion

1 cinnamon stick

1 sprig thyme

60 ml (2 fl oz) olive oil

1 tablespoon Chermoula
(see page 8)

4 shallots, peeled and
finely sliced

1 bunch spinach leaves

4 cloves garlic, sliced

2 tomatoes, seeded and diced

100 g (3½ oz) Bulgarian fetta

lemon wedges

Middle Easterners love lentils for their soothing starchiness and because they act as the perfect backdrop for all kinds of jazzing up with herbs, spices and aromatics. For this simple sauté, we like to use ultra-chic Puy lentils. These tiny slate-blue pulses are very pretty, and maintain their texture and shape very well.

This is the sort of simple but extremely tasty dish we like to eat on a cold, grey winter's evening, perhaps with a dish of slippery green lemon-spiked silverbeet on the side, or a salad of strong green leaves. It is also delicious served cold as part of a mezze selection.

Place the lentils in a large saucepan with three times their volume of cold water. Add the onion, cinnamon stick and thyme and bring to the boil, then lower the heat and simmer uncovered for 20 minutes, or until the lentils are just tender. Strain off the water and reserve the lentils.

In a frying pan heat the olive oil until sizzling hot. Add the chermoula, shallots and spinach, stirring to mix everything together. You want the chermoula paste to hit the hot oil, but not to burn – the spinach and onions help to lower the temperature.

As the spinach starts to collapse, add the garlic and tomatoes. Tip the lentils into the mix and stir well. Still on high heat, allow the mixture to cook for about 2 minutes, then remove from the heat and stir in the crumbled fetta. Taste and adjust the seasoning if necessary. Serve the lentils with lemon wedges.

SERVES 4 AS A SIDE DISH, OR 2 AS A LIGHT MEAL

poultry

Chicken Baked
with Almond Crumbs

CRUMBING MIX

200 g (7 oz) fresh breadcrumbs

70 g (2¼ oz) parmesan, grated

1 teaspoon sumac

zest and juice of 1 lemon

150 g (5 oz) flaked almonds

1 x 1.2 kg (2.4 lb) corn-fed
or free-range chicken, or
4 Marylands

80 g (2½ oz) plain flour

salt and pepper

3 eggs

50 ml (1½ fl oz) water

80 ml (2½ fl oz) olive oil

Crumbed chicken must be one of the most popular dishes for a family supper. The only problem is that most chicken is bland, flabby and flavourless, hardly surprising given the appalling way the mass-produced birds are reared. Happily, it is getting easier to find free-range quality chooks these days, and we urge you to choose these – whether you do it out of conscience, or for the superior flavour of the birds.

Here, we mix little slivers of almonds into the crumbing mix, which makes the chicken pieces look pretty funky and adds crunch. Do try and find sumac, which is available from most Middle East speciality stores, as it really intensifies the lemony flavour.

To make the crumbing mix, put the breadcrumbs into a food processor with the parmesan, sumac, lemon zest and almonds and pulse briefly to mix the ingredients together – you don't want to break up the almonds too much, so don't get carried away. Tip the crumbs out into a shallow bowl.

Joint the chicken into 8 pieces, or cut each Maryland in half.

Preheat the oven to 180°C (350°F).

Mix the flour with the salt and pepper in a bowl. In a separate bowl, lightly whisk the eggs with the water. First dip the chicken pieces into the seasoned flour, then the egg wash and finally the crumbing mix, patting it carefully all over.

Heat the olive oil in a frying pan and sauté the chicken until each piece is golden brown all over. Because the almonds in the crumbing mix will burn quite easily, it is very important to keep the chicken moving in the pan.

Place the chicken on a baking tray and cook them for 20 minutes in the centre of the oven. When cooked, remove them from the oven and allow to rest for a few moments before serving with wedges of lemon and a creamy potato salad.

SERVES 4

Chicken Schnitzel
Fried in Cumin Butter

4 skinless, free-range
chicken breasts

80 g (2½ oz) plain flour

1 teaspoon sweet paprika

a generous pinch of
chilli powder

2 tablespoons olive oil

CUMIN BUTTER

1 tablespoon cumin seeds

100 g (3½ oz) unsalted
butter, softened

½ teaspoon freshly
grated nutmeg

¼ Preserved Lemon (see pages
20–1), skin only, finely diced
or the zest of 1 lemon

juice of ½ lemon

Schnitzels are probably best known in their Viennese incarnation, dipped in egg and breadcrumbs and fried to a crunchy golden brown. But the thin escalopes of veal or breasts of chicken are also delicious without their crumb coating. The added bonus of this cut is that it is incredibly quick to cook, and almost universally popular.

This recipe uses free-range chicken breasts, and the schnitzels take on a savoury, almost Indian, flavour from the warm spiciness of cumin.

Prepare the chicken by sandwiching each breast between greaseproof paper or cling film. Use a heavy rolling pin to flatten it out carefully and evenly. (The paper helps stop the flesh disintegrating). You want to aim for a fairly even thickness of about 1 cm (⅓ in).

To make the cumin butter, roast the cumin seeds in a hot frying pan for a few moments, moving them constantly to stop them burning. Grind in a mortar to a fine powder and sieve to remove the husks. Tip the softened butter into a mixing bowl and blend in the cumin, nutmeg, preserved lemon or zest, and the lemon juice.

Sieve the flour, paprika and chilli powder together to make a pretty pink dust.

Put half the cumin butter into a frying pan with half the olive oil and heat until it just starts to foam. Quickly dip 2 of the schnitzels into the flour and pop them into the pan. Cook for 2 minutes, then turn and cook for a further minute. Remove to a warm dish lined with paper towels. Add the rest of the olive oil and butter (reserving a tablespoon for later) and bring back to temperature. Cook the remaining schnitzels, then remove them from the pan to the warm dish.

Use a piece of kitchen paper to carefully wipe out the frying pan, then lower the heat and drop in the remaining lump of cumin butter. Melt it over a gentle heat and drizzle over the schnitzels. Serve with potato salad, minted cabbage salad or potatoes fried with bacon and onions.

SERVES 4

Chicken Roasted with Forty Cloves of Garlic and Merguez Sausages

60 ml (2 fl oz) olive oil

salt and pepper

1 x 1.2 kg (2½ lb) jointed corn-fed or free-range chicken, or 4 Marylands

1–2 whole heads garlic (or 40 cloves if you insist)

8 Merguez sausages

8 shallots, whole

8 small potatoes, or potato chunks, parboiled

4 tomatoes, halved

2 Hungarian peppers, halved, with the stalks still attached

1 teaspoon Taklia (see page 9)

a few sprigs of rosemary

10 strands saffron

juice of ½ lemon

100 ml (3½ fl oz) water or chicken stock

salt and pepper

In this well-known French peasant dish, garlic is cooked in its skin and becomes all velvety smooth and creamy, with none of the overwhelming pungency the title of the dish might suggest. In our view there is nothing better than squeezing out the hot garlic cream over the roasted bird, or smearing it onto bread. You don't have to be literal about counting out forty cloves, but do, at the very least, use a whole head. Little Merguez sausages are from North Africa, and are usually bright red with chilli and other spices, adding a further spicy dimension to the dish.

Preheat the oven to 200°C (400°F).

Heat the oil in a large ovenproof casserole dish. Season the chicken pieces with salt and pepper and sauté until golden. Remove from the pan.

Separate the cloves out of each head of garlic, leaving their thin papery skins on. Put the garlic into the pan with the sausages and put everything on the heat until both sausages and garlic colour lightly. Tip them out of the pan and keep with the chicken.

Turn the heat right up and add the shallots, potatoes, tomatoes, peppers, taklia and rosemary. Mix the saffron with the lemon juice and pour into the pan with the water or chicken stock. Stir so that everything is nicely combined.

Sprinkle the vegetables with a little salt and pepper and place the chicken on top. Tuck the sausages and garlic cloves in among the chicken and vegetables, and put the dish into the centre of the oven. Cook for 40 minutes, or until the chicken is done.

Bring the casserole dish to the table and serve the chicken immediately with a bowl of buttered rice or noodles and a green salad. Make sure you have plenty of crusty baguettes on hand for smearing with the garlic.

SERVES 4

Lemon Chicken Fricassee with Honey-cured Bacon

4 skinless, free-range chicken breasts

salt and pepper

80 ml (2^1/$_2$ fl oz) olive oil

10 button mushrooms, stalks trimmed

6 shallots, quartered

4 preserved artichokes, quartered

^{1}/$_2$ Preserved Lemon (see pages 20–1), skin only, finely diced

1 large tomato, skinned, seeded and finely diced

100 ml (3^1/$_2$ fl oz) white wine

150 ml (5 fl oz) light chicken or vegetable stock

100 ml (3^1/$_2$ fl oz) cream

juice of ^{1}/$_2$ a lemon

1 tablespoon Red Harissa (see page 16)

8 rashers bacon

1 tablespoon honey

1 tablespoon finely chopped parsley

All kinds of fricassees were popular in the 1970s as a dinner party favourite. Nowadays, though, they seem to have fallen out of favour – possibly because the idea of an egg-enriched, flour-thickened cream sauce goes against present-day notions of light and healthy eating.

It is a bit of a shame, as fricassees are quick to cook and are very tasty. In contemporary versions, such as the one which follows, there is very little cream – just enough, in fact, to bind the sauce together, and to keep the flavours intense and fresh.

Cut the chicken into medium-sized pieces and season lightly with the salt and pepper. Heat the oil in a frying pan, then add the chicken. Sauté for 15–20 minutes until golden brown and just cooked through.

Lift the chicken out of the pan and keep warm. Now put the mushrooms, shallots, artichokes, preserved lemon and tomato into the pan and pour on the wine. Turn up the heat and boil until the wine reduces by two-thirds. Gently move the vegetables around from time to time to stop them sticking and burning.

Preheat the grill (broiler) to its highest temperature.

When the wine has reduced, pour in the stock, then the cream, lemon juice and harissa. Stir gently, then return the chicken to the pan. Taste and adjust the seasoning if necessary – it should be nice and sharp and lemony, with a touch of warm spice from the harissa. Keep the fricassee simmering while you grill the bacon.

Lay the bacon rashers on a lightly oiled baking sheet and drizzle over the honey. Grill (broil) the bacon until it is crisp and golden, turning once.

Serve the fricassee topped with bacon, parsley and accompanied by buttered rice.

SERVES 4

Maple-roasted Quail

8 small quail

2 tablespoons olive oil

salt

MAPLE GLAZE

50 ml (1¹/₂ fl oz) pure
maple syrup

1 teaspoon fresh thyme leaves

¹/₄ teaspoon cardamom
seeds, lightly toasted and
coarsely pounded

¹/₂ teaspoon freshly ground
black pepper

We just can't go past quail, particularly marinated and grilled or baked. These lovely little plump-breasted birds are quick to cook and have a fine delicate flesh. The maple syrup is blissfully easy to prepare and has a lovely smoky depth, which works particularly well with quail's underlying sweetness.

Preheat the oven to 150°C (300°F).

To make the maple glaze, combine all the ingredients in a bowl.

Trim the quail of necks, wing tips and the drumstick knuckle. Split them down the backbone and flatten out. Wash the insides and pat them dry, then cut each quail in half.

Heat the olive oil in a frying pan. Season the quail with the salt and cook them in batches in the hot oil until the skins colour lightly. Then put the quail in a roasting pan, skin side up. Baste them liberally with the maple glaze and cook in the centre of the oven for 25–30 minutes.

Serve the quail with a green leaf salad, and perhaps a blob of garlicky Toum (see page 13).

SERVES 4

Chicken Tagine with Green Herb Couscous

1.2 kg (2½ lb) free-range chicken pieces on the bone, skin removed

½ teaspoon salt

½ teaspoon sweet paprika

100 g (3½ oz) plain flour

60 ml (2 fl oz) olive oil

SAUCE

40 g (1¼ oz) currants

2 tablespoons sherry

2 tablespoons olive oil

2 large onions, finely diced

2 cloves garlic, finely chopped

1 leek, finely diced

3 small bulbs fennel

1 teaspoon white pepper

1 teaspoon ground ginger

15 strands saffron, roasted and crushed

a drizzle of honey

6 green chillies, halved, seeded and scraped

400 g (14 oz) waxy potatoes, peeled and cut into 2 cm (¾ in) dice

500 ml (16 fl oz) chicken or vegetable stock

juice of 1 lemon

COUSCOUS

250 g (8 oz) couscous

2 tablespoons olive oil

¼ cup parsley leaves, finely chopped

¼ cup coriander (cilantro) leaves, finely chopped

a knob of unsalted butter

Something a little different. This dish flies in the face of tagine wisdom, as it is quick to make, rather than a long, slow braise, where everything collapses into an intense sauce. The result is light, with fresh clean flavours, and it looks a treat served with the green-flecked couscous.

Season the chicken pieces with the salt. Mix the paprika with the flour and dust the chicken.

Heat the olive oil in a large heavy-based pan, add the chicken pieces and sauté slowly until they are golden all over. Remove the chicken from the pan and keep warm.

To make the sauce, first soak the currants in the sherry for 10–15 minutes.

Heat the olive oil in a pan and sauté the onions, garlic, leek and fennel for 5 minutes, or until soft and translucent. Add the pepper, spices and honey and stir well. Add the green chillies and potatoes to the pan and pour on the stock. Bring to the boil, then lower the heat and simmer uncovered for about 15 minutes, or until the potatoes are just tender.

Drain the currants and add them to the pan with the chicken. Cook for a further 5 minutes, or until the chicken is just done. Stir in the lemon juice and season with extra salt if necessary.

Prepare the couscous according to the method on page 38. Keep warm until ready to serve, then stir through the finely chopped herbs and the butter.

To serve, pile the couscous into a large, shallow serving dish. If you can, coax it into a tagine-shaped mound. Arrange the chicken pieces around the central pile of couscous, then pour the sauce all around.

SERVES 4

Quail with Limes and Ras al Hanout

8 x 200 g (7 oz) jumbo quail

MARINADE

2 cloves garlic, crushed with ½ teaspoon salt

juice and zest of 1 lime

1 teaspoon Ras al Hanout (see page 3)

salt and pepper

2 tablespoons olive oil

1 teaspoon honey

Another superb quail recipe! Here the little birds are rubbed in a tangy, spicy paste and left overnight for the flavours to permeate the flesh.

Trim the quail of their necks and wing tips, then split them in half down the backbone, and neatly slice out the breastplate (sternum) in the middle. Be careful not to cut completely through the flesh and skin of the bird. Clean the birds and pat them dry.

To make the marinade, combine all the ingredients in a large bowl. Place the birds in the marinade and rub it all over, thoroughly working into all the cracks and crevices. Ideally the birds should rest, covered, in the mixture overnight, or at least for a couple of hours.

To cook, season the birds with a little salt and pepper. Lift the quail out of their marinade and grill them wet on a griddle or on your barbecue. Cook them for 3 minutes, skin side down, then flip them over and cook for a further 3 minutes. As there is honey in the marinade, be sure to keep an eye on the cooking – they will burn fairly easily.

SERVES 4 AS A MAIN COURSE

Roast Quail Stuffed with Rice and Nuts

8 x 200 g (7 oz) jumbo quail

2 tablespoons olive oil

2 bushy sprigs rosemary

salt and pepper

STUFFING

100 ml (3½ fl oz) olive oil

1 small onion, finely diced

250 g (8 oz) medium-grain rice

about 400 ml (14 fl oz) water or light stock

½ teaspoon allspice

¼ teaspoon ground cinnamon

1 teaspoon salt

2 bay leaves

40 g (1¼ oz) flaked almonds

40 g (1½ oz) pine nuts

1 tablespoon extra virgin olive oil

Rice and nuts are a much-loved combination throughout the Middle East. Toasted almonds and pine nuts are used to add a lovely crunchy garnish to all kinds of rice dishes, or they are mixed into rice stuffings, and flavoured with a little minced lamb and spices such as cinnamon and allspice.

This particular recipe is a simple one that Greg uses routinely as a stuffing for roast chicken. It is also delicious as a stuffing for little whole quail, which would be very impressive at a dinner party, individually plated, or piled high on a central serving platter.

To make the stuffing, heat a third of the olive oil in a medium-sized saucepan and gently fry the onion until it softens and turns a light golden colour. Add the rice to the pan and stir well to coat all the grains. Now pour on enough of the stock or water to cover the rice by two fingers' width. Add the spices, salt and the bay leaves, cover the pan and cook on a very low heat for 20 minutes, or until all the water has been absorbed and the rice is tender.

While the rice is cooking, fry the almonds and pine nuts in the remaining olive oil until golden brown. The almonds burn very easily, so stir them constantly.

When the rice is cooked, tip it out into a mixing bowl, remove the bay leaves, and fork it through with the extra virgin olive oil. Then mix in the nuts and let it cool down before you stuff the quail.

When you are ready to cook the quail, preheat the oven to 180°C (350°F).

Stuff each bird with 2–3 tablespoons of the stuffing – you should pack it in reasonably tightly. Secure the skin at the opening with a toothpick and tie the legs together over the parson's nose.

Pour a little olive oil into a large roasting tin and brush the rest over the birds. Strip the rosemary needles from the twigs and scatter over the birds, then sprinkle with salt and pepper. Put the tin in the centre of the oven and cook for 10 minutes. Then pull the birds out of the oven, baste with the pan juices and return to the oven cook for a further 10 minutes.

Cover the birds with foil and let them rest for a good 5 minutes before you serve them with a dollop of plain yoghurt or a nutty Tahini–Yoghurt Sauce (see page 12) and a nice mixed green salad. These little birds are also delicious accompanied by a big blob of sticky Eggplant Jam (see page 24).

SERVES 4 AS A MAIN COURSE

Crisp Egyptian Pigeon with Coriander Salt

4 x size 7 pigeon

2 tablespoons Coriander Salt (see page 2)

280 ml (9 fl oz) vegetable oil for frying

POACHING STOCK

2 large onions, quartered

2 cloves garlic, crushed

2 sticks celery, diced

1/2 teaspoon ground cinnamon

1 cinnamon stick

15 threads saffron

1 bullet chilli, split

3 pods cardamom, cracked

1 small bunch coriander (cilantro), including stems

3 tablespoons honey

3 litres (6 pints) water

3/4 teaspoon sea salt

In Hong Kong the Chinese are true masters of cooking birds such as pigeon and duck. While he was cooking there in the 1980s Greg learned the trick of rubbing salt into the birds' skins the day before cooking, so that it permeates the skin and helps make the final result even more fragrant and crisp.

The poaching stock used for the pigeon in this recipe is a real joy. Not only is it deliciously aromatic and a glorious golden colour, but it can be strained, frozen and recycled almost indefinitely.

Use a heavy knife to trim away the claws and cut off the wing tips. Pull away any feathers that are still clinging to the skin. Rub half the coriander salt into the pigeon, making sure you get into every little crack and crevice. Cover the birds and refrigerate them for at least 24 hours.

To make the poaching stock, put the onions and garlic into a saucepan with the celery, cinnamon powder and stick, saffron, chilli, cardamom, coriander and honey. Pour on the water, bring it to the boil and reduce by a third. Now add the pigeon and salt and return to the boil. Cover the pan and lower the heat, then simmer gently for 20 minutes. When testing to see if the meat is tender, pierce the leg rather than the breast. If there is a little resistance and the juices are a faint pink, then the birds are done.

When the pigeons are cooked, remove them from the poaching stock and allow them to steam dry in the open air for 10 minutes.

Dust the birds with the remaining coriander salt. Heat the oil until moderately hot in a wok and cook the pigeon, no more than 2 at a time, turning them around in the oil as they colour. After about 5 minutes they should have turned a glossy mahogany. Remove the birds from the oil and sit them on kitchen paper for a couple of minutes to drain away excess oil. Serve a whole bird per person as a main meal, with more of the coriander salt for dipping. Accompany the birds with Shredded Carrot Salad (see page 39) and, if you like, a drizzle of Toum (see page 13).

SERVES 4

Chilli-charred Squab

4 x size 4 pigeon

lemon or lime wedges

SPICE PASTE
2 cloves garlic, crushed with
1 teaspoon sea salt
1 teaspoon sweet paprika
1/2 teaspoon chilli powder
1/2 teaspoon ground cinnamon
1 tablespoon olive oil

Pigeon or squab (baby pigeon) are popular all over North Africa, especially in Egypt, where they are popular street food, grilled on charcoal barbecues. Pigeon's dark meat is lovely and gamey. Consequently, it can take robust flavours such as chilli and garlic, and marries well with warm spices such as cinnamon. Here the birds are spatchcocked, rubbed with a cinnamony, mildly hot spice mix and grilled on a high heat. It's as simple as that.

Use a heavy knife to trim the sad little claws from the birds' elbows, cut off the wing tips and pull off any feathers still clinging to the skin. Split the pigeon down the backbone, and discard any innards. Flatten them out with their insides facing upwards. Carefully run a knife down each side of the breastplate (sternum), then use a strong pair of scissors to cut it away from the wing joints on either side. Carefully prise out the breastplate, peeling it away from the flesh. If you are at unsure about doing this ask the butcher to do it for you! Wash the birds well, inside and out, and pat them dry.

To make the spice paste, stir the garlic paste with the spices and the olive oil to make a nice fragrant slush.

Use your fingers to rub the paste all over the pigeon, inside and out, making sure you get into all the little cracks and crevices. Cover, refrigerate and allow to sit overnight for the flavours to permeate the flesh.

When ready to cook, preheat your barbecue or griddle to its highest temperature. Cook the pigeon for 3 minutes, skin side down, then turn and cook for a further 3 minutes. We prefer pigeon to be cooked medium–rare, in which case it should be ready after about 6 minutes. Otherwise, cook the birds for a further 2–3 minutes, or until done to your liking. Serve them straight from the grill, with wedges of lemon or lime. Or accompany with a tangy dressing such as Toum (see page 13), Juniper Berry Dressing with Preserved Lemons (see page 15), Walnut–Pomegranate Dressing (see page 14) or the deliciously cooling Green Coconut Chutney (see page 22).

SERVES 4

Sautéed Duck Risotto

GLAZE

2 tablespoons honey

a splash of sherry

seeds from 2 cardamom pods, lightly crushed

1 teaspoon cracked black pepper, lightly crushed

1 teaspoon orange-blossom water

2 tablespoons olive oil

4 x 160 g (5^1/$_2$ oz) duck breasts, skin on

salt and pepper

RISOTTO

up to 1 litre (2 pints) chicken or vegetable stock, simmering

20 strands saffron

1 cinnamon stick

60 ml (2 fl oz) olive oil

1 small onion, quartered

400 g (14 oz) Vialone Nano rice

60 ml (2 fl oz) white wine

100 g (3^1/$_2$ oz) fresh peas

1 tablespoon chopped parsley

1 tablespoon chopped celery leaves (from the heart)

100 g (3^1/$_2$ oz) unsalted butter, chilled and diced

60 g (2 oz) parmesan, grated

salt and pepper

This is a combination that works surprisingly well. The richness of the duck meat perfectly complements the risotto, which is fragrant and spicy, rather than overly rich and creamy.

To make the glaze, warm the honey gently with the sherry. Stir in the cardamom and pepper and add the orange-blossom water.

Heat the oil in a roasting pan until hot. Score the duck skins with a very sharp knife, season them with salt and pepper and place them, skin side down, in the pan. Lower the heat and cook until the skin turns a lovely golden brown, and the fat starts to render – it should take about 4 minutes. Turn the duck breasts over and cook them for a further 2 minutes. Tip off the rendered fat from the pan and brush the skin with the glaze. Turn the breast, skin-side down again, and cook for a final 2 minutes. Remove from the heat to rest and keep warm.

To make the risotto, bring the stock to the boil, then add the saffron and cinnamon stick and lower to a simmer. Heat the olive oil in a pan. Fry the onion for a few minutes to flavour the oil, then discard it. Add the rice and stir for a few minutes to coat each grain with the oil. Pour in the wine and bubble away until it evaporates. Next, ladle in enough simmering stock to cover the rice by a finger's width. Cook on medium heat, stirring with a wooden spoon from time to time, until most of the stock has been absorbed.

Add the same quantity of stock. Again, cook on medium heat, stirring from time to time, until most of the stock has been absorbed.

Add a third amount of stock (reserve around 100 ml/3^1/$_2$ fl oz for the final stage) and when half of the liquid has been absorbed, add the peas, parsley and celery leaves. Stir gently until the stock is all absorbed.

Mix in the butter and parmesan and season with salt and pepper. Add the final 100 ml (3^1/$_2$ fl oz) of stock and stir until the butter and cheese have melted. Cover the pot and allow to rest off the heat for a few minutes. Taste and adjust the seasoning if needed.

To serve, ladle out a nice mound of risotto into each bowl, slice each duck breast into 5 pieces and stack on the top. Serve with a peppery watercress salad and Juniper Berry Dressing with Preserved Lemons (see page 15).

SERVES 4

Duck Shish Kebab

4 x 200 g (7 oz) duck breasts, skin on, cut into 8 nuggets

3 smallish purple onions, quartered

2 tablespoons olive oil

MARINADE

1 teaspoon cardamom seeds

1 tablespoon sea salt

1½ teaspoons ground cinnamon

1 teaspoon ground nutmeg

1 teaspoon ground white pepper

1 teaspoon ground cloves

½ teaspoon ground black pepper

2 dried bay leaves, crumbled

2 purple onions, grated

2 cloves garlic, crushed to a paste

juice of 1 lemon

50 ml (1½ fl oz) white wine vinegar

Although lamb or chicken are the most popular meats for kebabs, duck is actually a terrific choice. It has a nice firm flesh, fabulous rich flavour and a good fatty skin, which lubricates the meat during the fierce cooking process. Marinate the duck for at least 24 hours ahead of time for maximum flavour.

To make the marinade, put the cardamom and salt into a mortar and grind to a fine powder. Tip into a large mixing bowl, add all the remaining dry spices and combine well. Toss the duck pieces into the spices and coat well.

In another bowl, mix together the onions, garlic, lemon juice and vinegar and stir well. Pour over the duck pieces, cover and leave to marinate for 24 hours.

When ready to cook, preheat the barbecue or grill (broiler) to its hottest temperature.

Separate the onions into layers.

We use metal skewers to cook the duck. You can use bamboo skewers, but presoak them for about 10 minutes before using so they do not burn. To assemble the skewers, start with a slice of onion, then thread on a piece of duck. Continue to thread onion and duck until you have 8 pieces of each per skewer. Try to keep the duck skin facing the same way and the onion slices all going the same way. Brush with olive oil and put on the barbecue. Cook, skin side down first, for about 2 minutes. Don't worry if the skin darkens and looks as if it's burning – this is normal. Then turn the skewers and cook for a further 2 minutes. Finally, turn back to the skin side and cook for a final minute for a crispy finish.

Serve with warm Arabic bread, Pickled Green Chillies (see page 23), salad and Tahini–Yoghurt Sauce (see page 12) or pungent, garlicky Toum (see page 13).

SERVES 4

meat & offal

Roast Leg of Lamb with Baharat and Root Vegetables

2 cloves garlic, crushed with
1 teaspoon sea salt

1 tablespoon Baharat
(see page 2)

1 lemon

1 kg (2 lb) leg of lamb

80 ml (2½ fl oz) olive oil

6 shallots, whole

12 small potatoes, or
potato chunks

3 parsnips, halved

12 wedges of swede

6 cloves garlic

a few sprigs of rosemary

1 teaspoon sea salt

Everyone's favourite family dinner, roast leg of lamb can sometimes do with a bit of jazzing up. There is a rich sweetness to the meat, which lends itself very well to the savoury spices of the Middle East and North Africa. Chermoula and harissa, with their chilli heat, work really well. Here, we opt for baharat, a common all-purpose spice blend in the Middle East of which every Lebanese housewife has her own. The aromas that waft around the house when cooking this roast are simply irresistible.

Preheat the oven to 220°C (425°F).

Mix the garlic paste with the baharat. Cut the lemon in half and rub it all over the lamb. Use your fingers to massage the spice paste all over the meat, making sure you get into all the cavities.

Put half of the olive oil into a baking dish, add the lamb and cook in the centre of the oven for 20 minutes. Turn the oven down to 180°C (350°F) and cook the lamb for a further 20 minutes. Now take the dish out of the oven and pour the rest of the oil into the base of the pan. Add all the vegetables, garlic and rosemary and sprinkle with a little salt. Shake them around as well as you can to coat with the oil. Put the pan back in the oven and cook for another 40 minutes. Check from time to time and turn the vegetables around in the pan to make sure they cook evenly.

The 80 minutes' cooking time will give a medium–rare result. Allow the meat to stand for a good 10 minutes before carving and serving with the pan juices.

SERVES 6

Lamb Baked with Orzo Pasta, Tomatoes and Lemon

60 ml (2 fl oz) olive oil

1.5 kg (3 lb) lamb leg, cut into 4 cm (1½ in) pieces

salt and pepper

2 large onions, diced

1 tablespoon Taklia (see page 9)

1 teaspoon sweet paprika

1 Preserved Lemon (see pages 20–1), skin only, roughly chopped

1 tablespoon honey

2 chillies, seeded, scraped and roughly chopped

2 x 400 g (14 oz) cans tomatoes

2 cinnamon sticks

juice of 1 lemon

1–1.5 litres (2–3 pints) light stock or water

500 g (1 lb) orzo pasta

150 g (5 oz) haloumi cheese, grated

Greek in inspiration, this is one of the tastiest and easiest supper dishes you could imagine. It is full of lemony, tomatoey flavours and has the added virtue of being just the kind of one-pot cooking that suits most people's busy schedules. The addition of grated haloumi at the end of the cooking time gives a lovely gooey finish.

Heat the oil in a frying pan. Season the lamb pieces with salt and pepper and sauté them, a few at a time, until lightly brown all over. Tip them into a large heavy-based casserole dish as you go. Now put the onions into the frying pan. Add the taklia and cook gently until the onions soften. Add the paprika, preserved lemon, honey and chillies and continue to stir over the heat.

Preheat the oven to 180°C (350°F).

Tip the spicy onion mixture on top of the lamb in the casserole dish and stir well. Pour in the tomatoes, add the cinnamon, lemon juice and 500 ml (16 fl oz) of the stock. Raise the heat and when the liquid is bubbling, put the casserole dish into the centre of the oven, cover and cook for 40 minutes.

Remove from the oven and add the orzo and an additional 500 ml (16 fl oz) stock, mixing everything together well. Pop the dish back into oven, uncovered this time, for a further 25 minutes. Stir occasionally to make sure it doesn't stick to the bottom of the pan. At the end of that time, check that the pasta is cooked and the lamb tender. If necessary, add a little more stock and cook for a further 10 minutes.

Remove the dish from the oven and turn the grill (broiler) to its highest setting. When it is really hot, sprinkle the casserole with the haloumi and pop under the grill until it melts. Serve immediately with some hot crusty bread and butter, and a fresh green salad.

SERVES 4

Lamb Kibbeh Stuffed with Mozzarella and Pine Nuts

KIBBEH SHELL

200 g (7 oz) fine-grade white
burghul (cracked wheat)

600 g (20 oz) lamb, minced twice

1 onion, puréed in a
food processor

¾ teaspoon allspice

½ teaspoon ground cinnamon

¼ teaspoon chilli powder

salt and pepper

FILLING

150 g (5 oz) mozzarella

80 g (2½ oz) pine nuts

1 tablespoon olive oil

½ onion, finely diced

¼ teaspoon allspice

2 tablespoons finely
chopped parsley

150 ml (5 fl oz) vegetable oil

Kibbeh are those little torpedo-shaped meat dumplings that, once upon a time, were the yardstick by which all Middle Eastern cooks were judged. They are a speciality of Syria and Lebanon, where marriages have been made and reputations destroyed, depending on the skill of the cook.

The traditional version consists of a thin crispy shell made out of a paste of burghul wheat and lamb, which is stuffed with a finer mixture of spiced lamb and deep-fried to a golden brown. This untraditional version is filled with molten cheese. They are a little fiddly to make, but you don't really need years of apprenticeship to a Lebanese housewife to achieve a passable, if not exceptional, result.

To make the shell, begin by soaking the burghul in plenty of cold salted water for about 10 minutes. Using your hands, squeeze out as much water as you can.

Put the lamb into a mixing bowl with the onion, burghul, the spices and the salt and pepper. Use your hands to mix everything to a soft smooth paste. You may need to add a little cold water to help bind everything together. Place the bowl in the refrigerator for 30 minutes, which makes the paste easier to work with.

While the lamb mixture is chilling in the fridge, prepare the filling. First, grate the mozzarella cheese. Fry the pine nuts in the olive oil until they are golden brown, then drain them on kitchen paper. Add the onion to the oil in the frying pan and sauté gently for a few minutes until softened. Tip the onion into a bowl and stir in the cheese, pine nuts, allspice, parsley and salt and pepper.

Take a small lump of the lamb paste into the palm of your left hand and roll it to a smooth ball. Using the forefinger of your right hand (reverse hands if you're left-handed), make an indentation in the lump and start to shape it into a hollow shell.
Try to make it as thin and even as you can. Fill the shell with about a teaspoon of the stuffing, wet the edges of the opening with cold water, and pinch it closed. You are aiming for a small torpedo shaped dumpling, with slightly tapered ends. Leave the stuffed kibbeh on a tray, covered, in the refrigerator until you are ready to cook them.

You can bake them in a 190°C (375°F) oven for about 20 minutes (the more virtuous option) or deep or shallow-fry them in medium–hot oil, turning to ensure a deep golden brown colour all over. Drain them on kitchen paper and serve hot with Toum (page 13) or Tahini–Yoghurt Sauce (page 12).

SERVES 4

Shish Kifte
(Minced Lamb Kebabs)

500 g (1 lb) lamb, minced twice

1 onion, grated

½ cup parsley, finely chopped

1 teaspoon dried mint or
2 tablespoons finely chopped
fresh mint

½ teaspoon freshly ground
black pepper

½ teaspoon Ras al Hanout
(see page 3, optional)

1 teaspoon sea salt

50 ml (1½ fl oz) olive oil

It's funny how mince means such different things to different people. To those of us with an Anglo-Saxon background, mince means, at best, hamburgers, and at worst a grey, watery, gristly slop. In the Middle East, however, mince is transformed by careful spicing to a thing of wonder. We particularly like it for making tiny tasty meatballs, or squashed into sausage shapes around skewers and grilled over hot coals.

Anyone who has visited the Eastern Mediterranean or Middle East will have fond memories of the savoury aroma of sizzling lamb kebabs. They are quick, easy and inexpensive to make, and are ideal for a barbecue, or for the kids' supper.

If you buy minced lamb from the supermarket, don't opt for the new 'lean' version – you need a reasonable fat content both for flavour and to help the kifte maintain their shape. If you get the lamb from a butcher ask for it to be minced twice, which makes for a smoother, finer result.

Mix together all the ingredients, except the olive oil, in a large mixing bowl. Knead well to a homogeneous sticky paste. Cover and refrigerate for at least an hour.

When ready to cook, preheat the barbecue or griddle to its highest temperature. If you are using wooden skewers, soak them for 10 minutes in cold water to stop them burning and catching fire.

Wet your hands, take a handful of the mince and shape it tightly around a skewer to make a long sausage about 10 cm (4 in) long and 3 cm (1½ in) in diameter. Keep going until you have used up all the mince.

Brush each kebab lightly with olive oil and grill on the barbecue or griddle plate. They will take anywhere between 5 and 8 minutes, depending on how well done you like them.

Serve them wrapped in warm Arabic bread, with a blob of Tzatziki (page 67) or Toum (page 13), and some salad leaves if you like.

SERVES 4

Oxtail Braised with Cinnamon and Preserved Lemon

3 kg (6 lb) oxtail, cut into pieces

1 generous tablespoon ground ginger

150 g (5 oz) plain flour

80 ml (2¹/₂ fl oz) olive oil

2 large onions, roughly diced

3 cloves garlic, finely chopped

4 sticks celery, roughly chopped

1 teaspoon ground cinnamon

1 Preserved Lemon (see pages 20–1), skin only, diced

8 cloves

1 teaspoon sweet paprika

2 x 400 g (14 oz) cans crushed tomatoes

100 g (3¹/₂ oz) pitted green olives

400 ml (14 fl oz) gutsy red wine

2 bay leaves

peel of ¹/₂ orange

around 500 ml (16 fl oz) stock or water

Oxtail is a favourite winter dish – all sticky-sweet and richly tender strips of gelatinous meat which, when cooked long enough and slow enough, fall away from their little knuckle of cartilage. A further bonus of this type of dish is that it requires minimal effort on the cook's part. Once the preparation is done, all you do is pop it in the oven and leave it well alone.

Preheat the oven to 160°C (325°F).

Get the butcher to trim any large lumps of fat away from the oxtail for you, and cut it through into nice little sections about 5 cm (2 in) long.

Mix the ginger into the flour and dust the oxtail pieces.

Heat the oil in a large heavy-based casserole dish and then brown the meat all over. Once coloured, remove the meat pieces from the pan. Add the onions, garlic and celery with the cinnamon, preserved lemon, cloves and paprika. Stir until everything is well mixed. Add the tomatoes, olives and splash in the wine. Tuck in the bay leaves and orange peel and return the oxtail to the tomato base. Pour in enough stock or water to just cover the meat, raise the heat and bring to the boil.

Cover the casserole and put it in the middle of the oven. Leave it for an hour, then remove it from the oven and stir everything around gently. Return it to the oven and cook for a further hour, by which time the meat will be a lovely glossy dark brown, and the sauce will have reduced to a sticky glaze. Serve with a big bowl of garlicky mashed potatoes.

SERVES 4

May's Vine Leaves with Mint Labne

1 kg (2 lb) vine leaves

300 g (10 oz) medium-grain rice

500 g (1 lb) minced lamb

1 teaspoon allspice

1/2 teaspoon ground cinnamon

salt and pepper

4 lamb chops from the neck
(or chump chops)

1 head garlic, cloves peeled

750 ml (24 fl oz) water

juice of 2 lemons

1 recipe Mint Labne
(see page 67)

Ask any good Lebanese boy what his favourite home-cooked dish is, and the chances are that he will nominate his mum's stuffed vine leaves. This is Greg's mother's recipe, which we both love, not just because it tastes delicious, but because of the neat way in which both the first course and meat course are prepared together in one large pot.

The idea is simple: after filling the vine leaves with a traditional rice stuffing, they are placed on top of lamb chops in a large pot. During the cooking process, all the bubbling juices rise to impregnate the stuffed vine leaves. These you eat first, with plenty of creamy yoghurt, and then follow with the meat course.

If using preserved vine leaves, soak them well, then rinse and pat dry. Fresh vine leaves should be blanched in boiling water for 30 seconds and refreshed in cold water.

Wash the rice and mix it with the lamb, spices, salt and pepper.

Lay the vine leaves out on a work surface, vein side up, and slice out the stems. Place a spoonful of the filling across the base of the leaf. Roll it over once, fold in the sides and continue to roll it into a neat sausage shape. The dolmades should be around the size of your little finger – don't roll them too tightly or they will burst during the cooking. Continue stuffing and rolling until the filling is all used.

Lay the lamb chops on the bottom of a heavy-based casserole dish, then pack the vine leaves in tightly on top, stuffing the garlic cloves in among them. Pour in the water and lemon juice, and place a plate on top to keep them submerged in the liquid. Slowly bring to the boil, then lower the heat and simmer gently for an hour.

The vine leaves can be eaten hot, warm or even cold. If serving them hot, carefully take them out of the pot and arrange them in a pile on a serving dish. Lay the lamb alongside to be eaten with or after the vine leaves.

If you plan to eat the dish cold, cool everything completely in the casserole dish. The whole thing will solidify into a lump. When cold, run a knife around the side of the dish, then invert it, a bit like a cake, onto a serving dish and allow everyone to help themselves.

Hot, cold or warm, serve the vine leaves and chops with plenty of Mint Labne (page 67).

SERVES 4

Veal Cutlets with Pine Nuts, Rosemary and Orange Crumbs

CRUMBING MIX

180 g (6 oz) pine nuts, toasted and roughly crushed

250 g (8 oz) breadcrumbs

zest of 1 orange

1/3 cup finely chopped rosemary

1/4 cup finely chopped sage

80 ml (2 1/2 fl oz) olive oil

3 eggs

60 g (2 oz) parmesan, grated

200 g (7 oz) plain flour

salt and pepper

8 veal cutlets

Crumbing mixes are a simple and effective way of transforming all kinds of meat and poultry dishes, especially pork and veal, which are, in our view, often rather bland. The crumb used here combines the lovely, mildly resinous flavour of toasted pine nuts with sweet orange and herbs. It is probably just cheesy enough to be popular with the kids, too.

To make the crumbing mix, place all the ingredients in a large mixing bowl and combine well.

Pour a generous pool of the oil into a baking dish and put it in the oven while you preheat it to 200°C (400°F).

In a shallow bowl, lightly whisk the eggs and cheese to make an eggwash.

Now, create a little assembly line of a shallow dish of flour seasoned with salt and pepper, a bowl with the eggwash and a shallow dish of crumbing mix. Dust each cutlet with flour, then dip into the eggwash, followed by the crumbing mix. You are aiming only to crumb the meat, not the bones.

Place the cutlets in the hot baking dish and sprinkle with the remaining oil. Put them in the centre of the oven and cook for 10 minutes. Turn them over and cook for a further 10 minutes. Serve the cutlets with a potato salad and maybe a drizzle of Green Harissa (see page 15). Or, if you want to develop the citrus theme a little further, then serve the cutlets with Baby Spinach Leaves with Citrus Fruits and Crushed Pine Nuts (see page 50), or try a simple green salad and add a squeeze of fresh orange juice to the vinaigrette.

SERVES 4

Pork Roasted with Black Pepper and Cinnamon

1 tablespoon black peppercorns
$1/2$ teaspoon ground cinnamon
2 cloves garlic
1 teaspoon sea salt
50 ml ($1^{1}/_{2}$ fl oz) olive oil
1.2 kg ($2^{1}/_{2}$ lb) loin of pork
1 teaspoon sea salt, extra

Roast pork is undoubtedly a firm family favourite, especially when it comes with its golden armour of tasty crackling. Sadly, most pigs these days are reared to be low fat and the meat has lost most of its flavour. If you can get an organically reared product you will have a much porkier and infinitely superior flavour.

The rather bland flavour of the lean pork is really zipped up by a mouth-tingling hit of aromatic pepper and comfortingly sweet cinnamon. For this dish we use a cut of pork called scotch fillet, which is the extension of the loin, and often comes oven-ready: trimmed, rolled and tied neatly with string. But do look for a piece that still has a thin layer of white fat– you don't want it stripped completely of its fatty layer as this creates important lubrication during the cooking process.

Slow-cooking allows the flavours of the marinade to meld into the meat. The moisture from the olive oil and water helps create some steam in the oven, which prevents it becoming stringy and dry.

Roughly crush the peppercorns in a mortar and pestle. Set aside. Put the cinnamon into the mortar with the garlic and salt and pound to a smooth paste, then mix in the pepper and half the olive oil.

Preheat the oven to 220°C (425°F).

Rub the paste all over the pork and allow it to sit while preheating the oven. Then sprinkle with the sea salt, which adds a lovely salty crunchiness to the crust.

Put the remaining olive oil into a roasting pan with 200 ml (7 fl oz) water to stop the bottom burning.

Cook for 20 minutes, then lower the oven to 160°C (325°F). Add another 200 ml water to the pan and cook slowly for a further hour.

When ready, remove from the oven, cover with foil and leave in a warm place to rest for 8 minutes. Serve with its pan juices reduced with a few knobs of butter, a big bowl of creamy mashed potato and some creamed spinach or green beans sprinkled with sumac.

SERVES 4

Pork Rib-eye with Caraway, Honey and Lime

3 cloves garlic, crushed with
1 heaped teaspoon sea salt

1/2 teaspoon cracked black pepper

1 teaspoon caraway seeds

1 x 1.5 kg (3 lb) pork rib-eye
(you want 6 ribs)

50 ml (1 1/2 fl oz) olive oil

1 litre (2 pints) water

GLAZE

zest and juice of 1 small lime

3 tablespoons honey

There is something wonderfully impressive about pork rib-eye, which makes it a terrific option for a dinner party or celebration. Its flavour is good, for today's low-fat porkers, and you can cook it with or without its crackling. In this dish, the meat is rubbed with a spice mix and glazed during the cooking process, so ask your butcher to remove the crackling for you. (You can always cook it separately.) While you're at it, make sure you ask for a piece from a smallish animal, with six ribs attached, and neatly tied.

Mix the garlic paste with the pepper and caraway seeds and rub this all over the meat. Use your hands and make sure you massage it into all the little nooks and crannies. Cover the meat and leave it in a cool place for an hour or so to allow the flavours to permeate.

Preheat the oven to 220°C (425°F).

Put the joint of pork into a large roasting tin, and wrap the sticking-up bones with tin foil to stop them charring in the heat. Pour the oil and water over the meat to create some steam and provide extra moisture during the cooking process.

Put the tin into the oven and cook for 20 minutes, then lower the heat to 160°C (325°F) and cook for a further hour and 20 minutes. Check every 30 minutes or so and splash in more water if necessary.

While the joint is cooking, make the glaze by heating the lime juice, zest and honey in a small pan, until it all melts together.

About 5 minutes before the end of the cooking time, take the joint out of the oven and turn the heat back up to 220°C (425°F). Brush the joint with the glaze and return it to the oven for the remaining 5 minutes or until it starts to caramelise a lovely bubbly brown.

To serve, cut into thick chops with a very sharp knife. Reduce the pan juices with a few knobs of butter and drizzle over the meat. Serve with roasted vegetables or a big bowl of creamy mashed potatoes.

SERVES 6

Black Pudding with Egyptian Fried Egg

4 eggs

plain flour for dusting

250 ml (8 fl oz) vegetable oil for frying

150 g (5 oz) Dukkah (see page 5)

1 black pudding, about 300 g (10 oz)

SALAD

1 bunch watercress, washed and stalks removed (about 3/4 cup leaves)

1 purple onion, finely shredded

1/2 teaspoon sumac

1 tablespoon extra virgin olive oil

juice of 1/2 lemon

Black pudding might not be everybody's cup of tea, but we adore its dark, rich and spicy meatiness. It is really worth hunting for the best quality pudding that you can find.

We offered a recipe for these Egyptian eggs in *Arabesque*, and make no apology for including them again here! The exotic fragrance of dukkah works so well with the sticky, richness of the egg yolks – and both are the perfect accompaniment to gorgeous black pudding. The eggs are also delicious in a salad.

Soft-boil the eggs for 3 minutes. Cool them under cold running water and peel carefully. Dust them in plain flour and then deep-fry each egg for 1–1½ minutes, or until they are golden-brown. Remove them from the oil and roll them in dukkah immediately.

Cut the black pudding into 12 slices, each about 1.5cm (2/3 in) thick, and dust with plain flour. Heat a little oil in a frying pan and sauté until brown on each side.

To make the salad, combine all the ingredients in a mixing bowl and toss well so that the leaves are nicely coated.

To serve, place a small mound of salad in the centre of each plate, and top with an egg. Arrange 3 slices of black pudding around the salad and drizzle with a little extra virgin olive oil and a sprinkle of extra dukkah. If you like, serve hot buttered toast on the side.

SERVES 4

Tiny Brain Omelettes with Mint and Gruyere

6 sets lamb's brains, soaked in milk for 2 hours, or cold salted water overnight

100 ml (3½ fl oz) vegetable oil

lemon wedges

POACHING LIQUID

1 lemon, quartered

1 cinnamon stick

4 cloves

½ onion

1 litre (2 pints) cold water

BATTER

2 large eggs

4 large egg yolks

6 spring onions (scallions), finely chopped

60 g (2 oz) gruyère, grated

30 g (1 oz) parmesan, grated

1 teaspoon dried mint

2 tablespoons finely shredded fresh mint

1 teaspoon salt

pepper to taste

This is a variation on a brain omelette that Greg's grandmother used to make as a treat for the family breakfast. In the Middle East, omelettes are quite different to the light fluffy French version. Known as *eggeh*, they are thick and densely cakey, stuffed full of vegetables, meat or chicken and usually flavoured with plenty of garlic and fresh herbs, such as mint.

Place the brains in a large saucepan with all the poaching ingredients. Bring to the boil, then skim and simmer for 2 minutes. Remove the pan from the heat and allow the brains to cool in the liquid. When they are cold, remove them from the liquid and split each set in half.

To make the batter, put the eggs and yolks into a mixing bowl and whisk lightly with the spring onions, both cheeses, fresh and dried mint and seasoning, just enough to bring everything together.

Slice the brains and add them to the batter.

Preheat the oven to 100°C (212°F) and put your serving dish in to warm.

Pour the oil into a frying pan and heat until moderately hot. Blob spoonfuls of the brain mixture into the hot oil, using an egg-ring as a mould if you have one. We used little cookie cutters which worked too, but you can just as well go for the free-form look. Cook the brains 3–4 at a time, frying until set and golden on the underside. Then carefully turn them over and fry on the other side. Be gentle, they are delicate! Remove from the oil and drain on kitchen paper, then keep them warm in the oven until all are cooked. Serve with lemon wedges.

SERVES 4 FOR BREAKFAST OR AS A STARTER

Lamb's Brains with Za'atar Crumbs, Bacon and Apple Butter

6 sets lamb's brains, soaked in milk for 2 hours, or cold salted water overnight

2 eggs

1 tablespoon water

100 g (3½ oz) plain flour

60 ml (2 fl oz) olive oil

8 rashers streaky bacon

lemon wedges

POACHING LIQUID

1 lemon, quartered

1 cinnamon stick

4 cloves

½ onion

1 litre (2 pints) cold water

APPLE BUTTER

200 ml (7 fl oz) apple juice

1 Granny Smith apple, peeled and grated

150 g (5 oz) cold unsalted butter, finely diced

salt and pepper

CRUMBING MIX

200 g (7 oz) dried breadcrumbs

100 g (3½ oz) parmesan, grated

1 teaspoon Za'atar (see page 4)

½ teaspoon sumac

Whether or not you can stomach offal is, we firmly believe, a result of your upbringing! Some people simply adore them, while others are revolted by the mere thought of eating an animal's internal organs. If you are predisposed to like them, then this dish is bound to be a winner. It is a wonderful balance of textures and flavours, combining the tender, creamy nuttiness of brains with tasty, salty bacon and a sweet fruitiness from the apple butter.

Place the brains in a large saucepan with all the poaching ingredients. Bring to the boil, then skim and simmer for 2 minutes. Remove the pan from the heat, and allow the brains to cool in the liquid. When they are cold, remove them from the liquid and split each set in half.

To make the apple butter, tip the apple juice into a pan and bring it to the boil. Simmer until reduced to 50 ml (1½ fl oz). On a low heat, add the grated apple to the syrup, and then tip in half the butter. Whisk until the butter melts into the syrup. As it melts, the syrup will thicken but don't allow it to froth up or boil. Keep it over a slow and steady heat until all the butter has melted, then slowly add the rest of the butter, bit by bit, whisking all the time to incorporate. Season with salt and pepper, then strain through a sieve and keep warm until needed.

Preheat the grill (broiler) to its highest setting.

To make the crumbing mix, combine the breadcrumbs with the parmesan, za'atar and sumac.

In a shallow dish, lightly whisk the eggs and water to make an egg wash.

Now get a little assembly line ready with a shallow dish with the flour, a dish with egg wash, and another dish of the crumbing mix. First dip the brains into the flour, then into the egg wash and then into the breadcrumbs. Continue until all are crumbed.

Heat the oil in a frying pan and fry the brains until golden brown.

Place the bacon on a baking tray and drizzle with a little of the apple butter. Grill (broil) until crisp and golden, turning once.

Serve 3 halves of brain per person, drizzle with a little apple butter and top with 2 pieces of bacon. Serve with lemon wedges on the side.

SERVES 4

seafood

Oysters with Lebanese Sausages

50 ml (1½ fl oz) olive oil

24 *mahannie* sausages

a squeeze of lemon juice

24 oysters, freshly opened

DRESSING

2 tomatoes, skinned, seeded and finely diced

3 shallots, finely diced

1 clove garlic, finely chopped

1 teaspoon pomegranate molasses

150 ml (5 fl oz) extra virgin olive oil

60 ml (2 fl oz) red wine vinegar

1 bay leaf

2 sprigs thyme

½ teaspoon sea salt

The combination of chilled briny oysters with tasty little plump pork sausages is a favourite in Northern France. Here we use chilli-hot, cinnamon-spiced Lebanese *mahannie* sausages. You will probably need to go to a Middle Eastern butcher for the sausages; try to find some that have a little chilli in them.

To make the dressing, combine all the ingredients in a mixing bowl and whisk together.

Heat the olive oil in a heavy-based frying pan and sauté the sausages over a medium heat for about 4 minutes. Turn them from time to time so they colour evenly, but be careful not to overcook. When they are ready, squeeze on the lemon juice and roll them around so that they are each coated with a little tangy acid.

Arrange 6 oysters on each plate. Cut the hot sausages in half on the diagonal and pop them on top of the oyster. Spoon over a little dressing and eat immediately.

SERVES 4

Grilled Scallops with à la Grecque Butter

20 scallops in their shell

BUTTER

150 g (5 oz) unsalted butter, softened

8 strands saffron, lightly roasted and crushed

1 teaspoon ground coriander

1 clove garlic, crushed with ½ teaspoon sea salt

1 tablespoon extra virgin olive oil

1 teaspoon white peppercorns, crushed

zest of ½ lemon

5 black olives, finely chopped

2 shallots, finely diced

Scallops in their shells are increasingly easy to find these days at decent fishmongers and require only very simple treatment.

Make the à la grecque butter by hand, or mix it very slowly in an electric mixer. You need it to be well combined, but don't want to get any air in.

Put the softened butter into the bowl of an electric mixer, add the remaining ingredients, and beat very gently until everything is well combined. Scrape it out onto a square of cling film and roll it neatly into a long thin log about the width of a 10-cent piece. Refrigerate until it sets firm.

Preheat the grill (broiler) to high. Place the scallop shells on a large baking tray (or do them in smaller batches). Cut the butter into thick rounds and drop one on top of each scallop. Place them under the hot grill for grill about 2 minutes, until just cooked through. Serve immediately with plenty of crusty bread to mop up the butter, and a perhaps a little mound of watercress to top each scallop.

SERVES 4 AS A STARTER

Scallops with Fried Olive Crumbs and Sumac

1 cup fresh breadcrumbs

80 ml (2½ fl oz) olive oil

10 large black olives, pitted and finely chopped

1 tablespoon chopped capers

1 teaspoon sumac

1 tablespoon finely chopped thyme leaves

zest of ½ lemon

1 tablespoon olive oil, extra

24 scallops

salt and pepper

lemon wedges

There is something infinitely seductive about these plump little molluscs, with their whiter than white flesh and startling orange coral. This is one of those almost perfect dishes, which seems to have just the right balance of textures and flavours. The scallops can be sweet, so the salty crunchiness of the olive crumbs creates just the right balance.

Preheat the oven to 180°C (350°F).

Scatter the breadcrumbs on a baking tray and drizzle the olive oil over them. Put in the oven and toast for 10 minutes until they become crunchy. Stir them around from time to time to stop them burning. Take them out of the oven and stir through the olives, capers, sumac, thyme and lemon zest.

To cook the scallops, heat the extra oil in a frying pan until it is smoking. Carefully place half the scallops in the pan, shake them around briefly, season with salt and pepper and let them sit for 30 seconds. Turn them over and cook the other side for a further 30 seconds, by which time they should be nearly cooked through. Remove them from the pan and cook the second batch of scallops in the same way.

Wipe the pan out and return to the heat, tip in the breadcrumb mixture and sauté for a minute until the crumbs are heated through. Return the scallops to the pan and cook with the crumbs for a final 30 seconds.

Serve straightaway, hot from the pan, with wedges of lemon.

SERVES 4 AS A STARTER

Tuna Kibbeh with Pickled Vegetables and Fresh Mint

300 g (10 oz) sashimi quality tuna, finely minced and chilled

1 large shallot, finely chopped

100 g (3¹/₂ oz) white, fine-grade burghul, rinsed in cold water and thoroughly drained

¹/₃ teaspoon allspice

1 bullet chilli, including seeds, finely chopped

1 teaspoon sea salt

pepper to taste

3 tablespoons extra virgin olive oil

TO SERVE

1 bunch fresh mint, divided into 4 lots

8 tiny pickled onions

4 Pickled Green Chillies (see page 23)

8 large black olives

4 large preserved artichokes, halved

4 pickled turnips

100 ml (3¹/₂ fl oz) very best quality extra virgin olive oil

Pickled vegetables are an essential part of the Lebanese mezze table, and in the Middle East many people make their own. You can buy a selection from a good deli, but try to get the best quality that you can find.

The tuna for this dish must be topnotch, and as fresh as a daisy. If you buy sashimi quality (which we suggest), it should already have the bloodline taken out. Otherwise you need to have it cut out, as it is bitter.

Traditionally kibbeh is made from very finely minced, lightly spiced raw lamb, and served with raw onion and fresh mint. It really works very well with seafood (salmon is good too), which is somehow more palatable to Western palates. The acid tang of the pickled vegetables helps to cut through the richness of the oily tuna, and also adds a good crunch.

Chill a stainless steel or glass bowl, and in it mix the tuna, shallot, burghul, allspice, chilli, salt, pepper and olive oil. Form into 4 flat oval shapes and refrigerate for a minimum of an hour.

When you are ready to eat, place an oval of the kibbeh in the centre of each plate. Use the back of a soup spoon to make little indentations down either side of an imaginary central spine. The idea then is to drizzle over extra virgin olive oil, which gathers in gleaming golden pools in the little hollows.

Refresh the mint in icy-cold water. Serve the kibbeh with the mint and pickled vegetables, or if you like, a little salad. Eat straight away with plenty of fresh Arabic bread, which you use to scoop up mouthfuls of the kibbeh and mint leaves.

Accompany with a blob of creamy Yoghurt Cheese (see page 31) or decorate with sumac if you like.

SERVES 4 AS A STARTER

Mussels, Leeks and Pernod with Taramasalata Toasts

2 kg (4 lb) mussels

80 ml (2½ fl oz) olive oil

3 leeks, white part only, finely shredded

3 cloves garlic, finely chopped

2 small bulbs fennel, halved, cored and thinly sliced

100 ml (3½ fl oz) Pernod

1 teaspoon Green Harissa (see page 15)

⅓ cup parsley, roughly chopped

1 tablespoon chopped celery leaves (from the heart)

150 ml (5 fl oz) thickened cream

½ baguette, sliced into rounds and toasted

100 g (3½ oz) Taramasalata (see page 63)

Some people are a little daunted by the idea of cooking mussels, until they actually try it and discover how simple the process really is. Many supermarkets and fishmongers today sell net bags of beautiful blue-black mussels, already scrubbed clean of their dirty beards. But even if you buy a loose heft of them, still dangling their seaweedy fronds, all they really need is a bit of vigorous scrubbing and tugging.

The cooking process itself requires absolutely minimum effort, and we just love the way the smell of the sea fills the air while the mussels are steaming. The taramasalata toasts just seem to be the perfect classy little accompaniment.

Scrub the mussels clean of any sand and dirt and pull away the beards (throw away any mussels that refuse to close after a sharp tap).

Heat the oil in a large cooking pot (such as a Le Creuset), and add the leeks, garlic and fennel. Stir around over a medium heat for a few minutes, then tip in the mussels and shake the pan to move them around over the heat. Pour in the Pernod, cover the pan, turn up the heat and steam for about 3 minutes. Shake the pan vigorously from time to time.

Remove the lid from the pan and stir the mussels around well, then put the lid back on and steam them for a further 2 minutes. Check and discard any mussels that haven't opened.

Add the harissa, parsley, celery leaves and cream. Bring to the boil and mix everything well.

Divide the mussels among 4 large bowls and spoon over the vegetables and juices. Take care to leave any gritty bits of sand in the pot.

Serve with sliced toasted baguette spread with taramasalata.

SERVES 4 AS A STARTER OR LIGHT LUNCH DISH

Baby Octopus Chargrilled with Moroccan Spices

2 tablespoons Chermoula (see page 8)

½ onion, finely diced

1 tablespoon roughly chopped coriander (cilantro) leaves

1 tablespoon roughly chopped parsley

1 tablespoon olive oil

300 g (10 oz) baby octopus, cleaned and dried

lemon wedges

This is one of those meals that are bound to bring back memories of hot summer nights and barbecues by the beach. Although you could cook the octopus on one of those ridged stovetop griddle plates, they really are better barbecued – the lick of flame is essential for a true smoky flavour, and to char the little tentacles properly.

Octopus are readily available, both fresh and frozen. The frozen stuff is usually already cleaned, but tends to be saltier, and therefore needs to be carefully rinsed. Although it is perfectly acceptable, it seems to be flabbier and soggier. Use fresh local octopus if you can get it. Most fishmongers will oblige with the cleaning.

In a mixing bowl, combine the chermoula with the onion, herbs and olive oil. Tip in the octopus and mix them around well with your hands, making sure the marinade coats every little bit. You can do this overnight if you like, but at least an hour ahead of time.

Heat the barbecue as high as possible. The octopus will take 3–4 minutes to cook. Throw them onto the hottest part of the barbecue and turn once during the cooking time – don't worry if they look a little black around the tentacles – you want them to come into contact with flame for that authentic chargrilled taste.

Serve the octopus straight from the flames with lemon wedges.

SERVES 4 AS A STARTER OR AS PART OF A BARBECUE

Atlantic Salmon Grilled with Fennel, Lime and Sumac

SPICE MIX

finely grated zest of 2 limes

$^1/_2$ teaspoon chilli powder

1 teaspoon fennel seeds, lightly roasted and crushed

2 teaspoons sumac

SALAD

1 bulb fennel, thinly sliced

1 purple onion, thinly sliced

$^1/_2$ teaspoon dried mint

60 ml (2 fl oz) extra virgin olive oil

juice of $^1/_2$–1 lime

100 g (3$^1/_2$ oz) fetta

2 tablespoons olive oil

4 x 160 g (5 oz) salmon medallions

The citrussy tang of lime and sumac and the zing of chilli are really good with the oiliness of the fish. Drying the zest makes it easier to mix in with the other spices.

To make the spice mix, dry the lime zest overnight, or put in a very low (about 75°C/160°F) oven for 30 minutes. (This intensifies the lime flavour.) Mix the lime zest with the chilli powder, fennel seeds, sumac and salt and pepper.

To make the salad, mix together the fennel, onion and dried mint. Whisk together the olive oil and lime juice and season with salt and pepper.

Now, heat the olive oil in a frying pan. Season the salmon pieces all over with the spice mix. Put in the pan and sauté for 1–2 minutes on each side so that it is evenly coloured. This should be enough to cook the salmon to medium–rare.

Dress the salad and crumble over the fetta. Divide among serving plates. Place the salmon on top of the salad, drizzle over a little extra virgin olive oil, and serve.

SERVES 4 AS A MAIN COURSE

Cumin-fried Whitebait

700 ml (23 fl oz) vegetable oil for deep-frying

200 g (7 oz) plain flour

$^1/_2$ teaspoon salt

3 tablespoons cumin seeds, lightly roasted, ground and sieved

1 teaspoon ground ginger

$^1/_2$ teaspoon ground white pepper

400 g (14 oz) whitebait

We find whitebait totally irresistible. Here, lightly seasoned with savoury cumin and deep-fried, they make a fantastically simple starter, served straight from the pan with lots of lemon wedges or a homemade preserved lemon mayonnaise.

Heat the oil in a deep-fryer or wok to 190°C (375°F), or until a cube of bread dropped in sizzles slowly to the top and turns golden brown in about 30 seconds.

Put the flour, salt, cumin, ginger and pepper into a large bowl and mix together well. Tip in the whitebait and toss them around in the seasoned flour until they are well coated. Then lift them out and shake off any excess flour.

Deep-fry the whitebait in batches for 2–3 minutes, until they are crisp and golden. Drain them briefly on kitchen paper, then tip into a large serving bowl and serve with fresh brown bread and butter, lots of lemon wedges and mayonnaise.

SERVES 4 AS A STARTER

Coriander-cured Salmon with Crushed Coriander Dressing

1 whole fillet Atlantic salmon, 1.2–1.5 kg (2$\frac{1}{2}$–3 lb), skin on, bones removed

250 g (8 oz) sea salt

200 g (7 oz) caster (superfine) sugar

2 tablespoons coriander seeds, crushed

1 tablespoon juniper berries, crushed

zest of 1 lemon

1 bunch coriander (cilantro), including roots

150 ml (5 fl oz) extra virgin olive oil

1 clove garlic, crushed with 1 teaspoon sea salt

juice of $\frac{1}{2}$ lemon

Given that you need a whole fillet of salmon for this dish, it is probably one that you will want to save for a special occasion. We tend to prepare it for Christmas and family birthdays as part of a mezze selection. It's very simple to prepare and all you need is a very sharp knife when it comes to slicing the fish into wafer thin slices.

The salmon is cured with salt and sugar, in much the same way as a gravlax. But instead of using dill, which is the Scandinavian tradition, we use coriander, juniper berries and lemon, which give it a citrussy flavour that cuts through the fish's densely rich oiliness.

Place the salmon fillet in a shallow dish. Mix together the sea salt, sugar, coriander seeds, juniper berries and lemon zest in a large mixing bowl. Chop the roots off the coriander and lay them over the salmon, then pack on the salt–sugar curing mix. Wrap the salmon in cling film and weigh it down lightly – a couple of plates will do the trick. Refrigerate for 12 hours, then remove the plates, turn the salmon upside down, and refrigerate for a further 6 hours.

After the 18 hours' curing time, peel the cling film off the salmon and wipe away the curing mix and coriander roots. Gently wash the cured salmon under cold water and pat dry. Rub it all over with 50 ml (1$\frac{1}{2}$ fl oz) of the extra virgin olive oil, cover and refrigerate again until needed. It will keep up to 7 days.

When you are ready to make the dressing, pick the leaves from the bunch of coriander and put them into a food processor with the garlic paste and a tablespoon of extra virgin olive oil. Blitz to a fine paste, adding the lemon juice and the rest of the oil.

To serve, slice the salmon very thinly and serve with the coriander dressing, lemon wedges, boiled new potatoes and a good strong oniony salad.

SERVES 12

Ceviche of Red Mullet with Ras al Hanout

8 x 150 g (5 oz) red mullet

2 tomatoes, seeded and very finely diced

2 mild green chillies, seeded, scraped and finely shredded

1 medium-sized purple onion, very finely sliced

1 cup coriander (cilantro) leaves, roughly chopped

1 clove garlic, crushed with $\frac{1}{2}$ teaspoon sea salt

juice of 3 limes

85 ml (2½ fl oz) good quality extra virgin olive oil

1 level teaspoon Ras al Hanout (see page 3)

salt and black pepper

You would be hard-pressed to find a simpler dish than ceviche, the traditional Mexican technique of 'cooking' fish with the acids from citrus fruit, in particular, limes. You can pretty much ceviche any seafood – all white fish work well, as do oily fish such as salmon and mackerel, and even molluscs, such as scallops.

Here we use red mullet, a lovely delicate fish that is enormously popular around the Mediterranean. Go to a good fishmonger to make sure that they are super-fresh. If you feel up to the task, clean and fillet the fish yourself, otherwise ask the fishmonger to do it for you. Explain what you are preparing, and ask the fishmonger to be as gentle as possible so as not to crush the delicate flesh. If you cannot find red mullet, use any other good white fish – whiting or garfish would work well.

First, scale the red mullet. Hold it under running water and use your thumb to run against the scales from tail to head. They are delicate and come away very easily. Then use a really sharp knife and carefully slice away the two fillets from the bones. Use tweezers to remove any little bones, being as gentle as you can so as not to mush the flesh.

In a large mixing bowl, combine the tomatoes, chillies, onion and coriander. Whisk the garlic paste with the lime juice, olive oil and ras al hanout. Pour the dressing into the bowl and mix everything together well. Taste and add a little extra salt if necessary.

Spoon half the marinade into the bottom of a shallow dish, spreading it out evenly, and lay the fish fillets on top, skin side up. Then spoon the rest of the marinade over the fish so they are completely covered. Lightly sprinkle with salt and black pepper, then cover the dish with cling film and refrigerate for an hour.

Serve with plenty of warm crusty bread, and perhaps a tomato salad.

SERVES 4 AS A STARTER

Rockling Braised with Arabic Spices and Angel Hair Pasta

4 x 180 g (6 oz) rockling fillets

$^{1}/_{2}$ teaspoon Baharat (see page 2)

salt and pepper

50 ml ($1^{1}/_{2}$ fl oz) olive oil

360 g (12 oz) angel hair pasta

a knob of unsalted butter

juice of $^{1}/_{2}$ lemon

BRAISE

250 g (8 oz) haricot beans

80 ml ($2^{1}/_{2}$ fl oz) olive oil

2 purple onions, sliced

2 cloves garlic, sliced

20 strands saffron, lightly roasted and ground

1 bullet chilli, finely chopped

4 tomatoes, quartered

1 x 5 cm (2 in) strip of orange peel

a few sprigs of thyme

200 ml (7 fl oz) chicken or vegetable stock

2 tablespoons extra virgin olive oil

Another easy one-pot dish that requires a few herbs and spices, but virtually nothing in the way of fancy fingerwork! You do need to remember to soak the beans overnight, however.

Rockling is ideal, as it is a firm-fleshed sweet fish, but you can just as easily use another similar fish: monkfish tails, rock flathead tails or even skate or freshwater eel if you are feeling adventurous. Try to get fillet pieces cut from the head end of the fish rather than the tail, as they are thicker and have a firmer texture.

First, soak the beans overnight and cook them in boiling water for about 30 minutes or until they are tender.

Preheat the oven to 220°C (425°F).

To make the braise, heat the oil in a heavy-based casserole dish. Add the onions, garlic, saffron, chilli and tomatoes and sauté for a few minutes on a high heat. Lower the heat and simmer for 5 minutes. Cut the fish into thickish strips, and season with the baharat and salt. Heat the olive oil in a frying pan, and sear the fish on all sides so that it colours nicely.

Put the casserole dish back on the heat, and add the beans to the braise with the orange peel and thyme. Place the fish pieces on top, pour on the stock and bring to the boil. Lower the heat and simmer for 5–7 minutes, or until the fish is just cooked through.

Towards the end of the cooking time, bring a pan of salted water to the boil to cook the pasta until al dente. Drain well, then stir through the butter, lemon juice and season with salt and pepper. Use a fork to twirl the pasta into little coiled mounds and serve on top of the fish with a generous spoonful of the braise.

SERVES 4 AS A MAIN COURSE

Grilled Snapper with Tahini-Yoghurt Dressing

1 recipe Tahini-Yoghurt Dressing
(see page 42), made without
the parsley and tomato

4 x 200 g (7 oz) snapper fillets

salt and pepper

80 ml (2½ fl oz) olive oil

extra virgin olive oil

a pinch of sumac

This recipe and the next are the sorts of fish dishes that are very popular in the Middle East. Tahini-yoghurt dressing is the classic accompaniment to cold fish. The earthiness of the tahini, combined with the lemony tang of the yoghurt, complements the soft richness of the fish superbly.

You need to use a firm-fleshed white fish such as snapper. Ask your fishmonger for two whole baby snapper, of about 700 g (23 oz) each, and get them filleted for you. Each fillet will be enough for one person as a main course. Use two frying pans, so you can cook all the fish at once.

Make the dressing according to the instructions on page 42.

Use kitchen paper to pat the snapper dry, then season lightly on both sides. Heat the oil in 2 frying pans until almost smoking, then lower the heat to medium-high and put the fillets in, skin side down. Fry for 2 minutes, then turn them over and fry for another 2 minutes. Remove from the pans, cover and allow to cool completely.

When the fish is cold, drizzle with a little extra virgin olive oil, then cover with the dressing. Serve sprinkled with a little sumac.

SERVES 4 AS A MAIN COURSE

Grilled Snapper with Walnut–Pomegranate Dressing

1 recipe Walnut–Pomegranate
Dressing (see page 14)

4 x 200 g (7 oz) snapper fillets

salt and pepper

80 ml (2½ fl oz) olive oil

a splash of extra virgin olive oil

Here, the fish is served piping hot, straight from the pan, and is accompanied by a thick, nutty sauce known around the Middle East as tarator. In Lebanon, tarator is usually made with pine nuts, but we use the more Turkish option of walnuts. Their dark toastiness works beautifully with the sour-sweet intensity of the pomegranate molasses.

Make the dressing according to the instructions on page 14.

Use kitchen paper to pat the snapper dry, then season lightly on both sides. Heat the oil in 2 frying pans until almost smoking, then lower the heat to medium–high and put the fillets in, skin side down. Fry for 2 minutes, then turn them over and fry for another 2 minutes.

Remove the fish from the pan and place on serving plates, skin side up. Drizzle with a little extra virgin olive oil, then spoon over the dressing. All this dish needs is some simple boiled new potatoes and a soft green-leaf salad.

SERVES 4 AS A MAIN COURSE

Fricasseed Prawns with Leeks and Saffron

12 raw king prawns in their shells, about 1 kg (2 lb)

1 tablespoon Ras al Hanout (see page 3)

60 ml (2 fl oz) olive oil

3 small leeks, white part only, cut into medium dice

1 clove garlic, finely chopped

2 small bulbs fennel, thinly sliced

a generous splash of white wine

15 strands saffron, lightly roasted and ground

500 ml (16 fl oz) chicken or vegetable stock

1 teaspoon Dijon mustard

100 ml (3$\frac{1}{2}$ fl oz) thickened cream

salt and pepper

juice of $\frac{1}{2}$ lemon

2 tomatoes, skinned, seeded and cut into medium dice

1 tablespoon chopped parsley

This is definitely a special occasion dish, with its glorious golden tones, luscious, velvety cream sauce and strong, heady flavours. This is a modern-day fricassee, without the traditional egg yolks for enriching. Instead, the sauce is reduced to an intensely sticky richness, and only needs some egg noodles or plain steamed rice to accompany it.

Peel the prawns and remove the heads, but leave the tails intact. With a sharp knife, split them along the back and carefully pull away the intestines. Rub the prawns all over with the ras al hanout and allow them to sit for an hour to marinate.

Heat the oil in a frying pan until sizzling hot. Sear the prawns very quickly on both sides, and then remove from the pan. Keep the heat high and add the leeks, garlic and fennel and toss them around the pan for a minute. Add a healthy splash of white wine to deglaze the pan, then add the saffron. Pour in the chicken stock, reduce the heat a little and allow to bubble away until the liquid reduces by two-thirds and the vegetables soften. It will probably take about 8 minutes or so.

When reduced, add the mustard and cream and stir in well. Bring the sauce back to the boil, taste and season with salt, pepper and lemon juice. Put the prawns back into the pan with the tomatoes, and cook for another minute, just so that prawns cook through. Sprinkle with parsley and serve with buttered noodles or plain rice and a soft green-leaf salad.

SERVES 4

vegetables

Artichokes with Avgolemono

8 large globe artichokes

POACHING STOCK
2 litres (4 pints) water
juice of 2 lemons
100 ml (3½ fl oz) white wine
2 tablespoons olive oil
3 cloves garlic, halved
2 bay leaves
⅓ bunch thyme
1 large onion, quartered
2 teaspoons salt

AVGOLEMONO
2 whole eggs
1 egg yolk
juice of 1 lemon
100 ml (3½ fl oz) hot
chicken stock
a pinch of sumac

Many contemporary recipes for artichokes use the central hearts only. While these little nuggets of nutty-sweet flesh are delicious, there is also a lot to be said for the good old-fashioned way of eating artichokes – one leaf at a time, scraping the prized flesh off between your teeth, and working your way towards the central heart. It does involves getting down and dirty at the table, with lots of pulling and dipping and dripping of sauce everywhere – but it's also a lot of fun and very more-ish.

Put all the ingredients for the stock into a large saucepan and bring to the boil. Lower the heat and simmer for 10 minutes.

To prepare the artichokes, pull off the hard outer leaves and use a vegetable peeler to shave away the rough outer layer of the stalk. Slice off the top quarter of the artichoke and discard.

Drop the artichokes into the simmering stock and cover them with a plate to keep them submerged in the liquid. Simmer for about 20 minutes, or until the stalks are tender. They will keep for 4–5 days in the cooking stock, and are delicious eaten cold. If you want to eat them hot, reheat them briefly in the stock. Remove them from the stock and leave them to drain upside down for a few minutes.

To make the avgolemono, in a small pan, whisk together the eggs and egg yolk with the lemon juice. In a separate pan, bring the stock to a simmer and add a spoonful of it to the egg mixture. Stir well, then pour the egg mixture into the barely simmering stock, whisking well all the time. Cook gently over the low heat, stirring constantly with a wooden spoon, until the sauce is thick enough to hold a line drawn across the back of the spoon. Remove from the heat and pour it into a bowl to accompany the artichokes.

SERVES 4

Sautéed Zucchini with Tzatziki

4 medium-sized zucchini (courgettes)

salt and pepper

50 g (1½ oz) unsalted butter

50 ml (1½ fl oz) olive oil

1 long green chilli, seeded, scraped and finely shredded

½ teaspoon dried mint

200 ml (7 fl oz) Tzatziki (see page 67)

A nice refreshing vegetable mezze dish in the summer, this simple sauté of zucchini is also nice as an accompaniment to cold meats. Cold minted tzatziki is a great dressing for all kinds of dishes, and here it picks up on the mint in the zucchini.

Trim the ends off the zucchini, cut in half lengthways and then into medium-sized chunks. Sprinkle with salt and put them into a colander for 20 minutes. This helps to reduce the quantity of oil they absorb while frying. Rinse the zucchini well and dry them thoroughly on kitchen paper.

Melt the butter in a frying pan with the olive oil and add the zucchini and chilli. Sauté over a medium heat until the zucchini is tender and evenly coloured all over. Sprinkle over the mint, lightly season with salt and pepper then tip into a serving dish. Serve hot with a big blob of tzatziki on the side, or cold as a refreshing salad.

SERVES 4

Creamed Fetta Spinach

50 ml (1½ fl oz) olive oil

2 shallots, finely diced

1 clove garlic, finely chopped

2 large bunches spinach, stalks removed and leaves shredded

80 ml (2½ fl oz) thickened cream

150 g (5 oz) good quality fetta, roughly crumbled

50 g (1½ oz) parmesan, grated

¼ teaspoon allspice

salt and pepper

The strong vital flavour of leafy vegetables such as spinach and silverbeet works brilliantly with other strong flavours such as caramelised onions, garlic, preserved lemon or chilli. We like this spinach dish as an accompaniment to all kinds of dishes. The fetta and nutmeg make it somewhat reminiscent of the Greek spinach pie, spanakopita.

Heat the olive oil in a large heavy-based pot. Add the shallots and garlic and stir over a medium heat for a few minutes until softened. Now turn the heat right up and immediately tip in the spinach. Stir around for a minute or so until the spinach collapses. Keep cooking over a high heat.

The spinach will start to give up moisture, which you should keep pouring off. When you think most of the liquid has evaporated, pour in the cream and swirl it around. As soon as the cream starts to bubble, add the fetta, parmesan, allspice, salt and pepper. Serve immediately.

SERVES 4 AS A SIDE DISH

Sautéed Fennel and Tomato Couscous

150 g (5 oz) couscous

¹/₂ teaspoon salt

200 ml (7 fl oz) boiling water

60 ml (2 fl oz) olive oil

2 large shallots, sliced

2 small bulbs fennel, cored and finely diced

2 tomatoes, finely diced

1 tablespoon shredded fennel leaves

8 black olives, pitted and sliced

1 tablespoon shredded mint leaves

¹/₂ teaspoon dried mint

1 teaspoon sumac

juice of 1 lemon

salt and pepper

A lovely refreshing lemony couscous dish that can be eaten hot or cold as a tabbouleh-like salad. Use the recipe as a base, and vary the flavourings. Try it with a touch of chilli or use different herbs – tarragon, basil or even plain old parsley would work well. Or, for another lemony dimension, toss through some finely diced preserved lemon.

Put the couscous and salt into a bowl and pour over the boiling water. Cover and leave for 15 minutes. Fluff up the grains with a fork and add a tablespoon of the olive oil, then cover again and set aside while you cook the vegetables.

Heat the remaining olive oil in a large frying pan and add the shallots and fennel. Sauté over a high heat for a minute, then add the tomatoes, fennel leaves, olives, fresh and dried mint and sumac. Keep the heat up high and stir-fry the vegetables until they start to colour.

Tip in the couscous and mix thoroughly. Sprinkle with the lemon juice, check for seasoning and serve immediately.

SERVES 4

Hungarian Peppers Cooked in Lemon Oil

LEMON OIL

250 ml (8 fl oz) fruity Spanish olive oil

2 whole lemons, quartered

1 tablespoon coriander seeds

1 tablespoon black peppercorns

2 bay leaves

1 cinnamon stick

8 Hungarian peppers

peel of 1 lemon

Hungarian peppers are a long and rather mild capsicum. When green, they have only a slight buzz of heat, but as the red blush of ripeness spreads along their length, the chilli heat intensifies. For this recipe, which is a kind of confit of peppers in a lemon-spiced oil, you want the mild green variety. Eat as a condiment with cold meats as part of a mezze selection, in salads or warmed through and served as a vegetable accompaniment to grills and roasts.

To make the lemon oil, put the oil in a large saucepan and heat gently to blood temperature. Put the lemons, coriander seeds, peppercorns, bay leaves and cinnamon stick into a bowl and pour on the olive oil. Leave to infuse overnight. If you want, you can strain and decant the oil into a bottle for use in salad dressings.

Preheat the grill (broiler) to its highest heat.

Lay the peppers out on a baking sheet and slide them under the grill. Cook for 10–15 minutes, turning from time to time, so that the skins blister all over.

Remove the peppers from the oven, allow them to cool a little, then peel away the skin. Split them in half, leaving the stalks attached at the top to hold them together, and scrape away the seeds.

Preheat the oven to 200°C (400°F).

Put the peppers into a shallow dish and add the lemon peel. Strain 100 ml (3$^{1}/_{2}$ fl oz) of lemon oil and pour it over the peppers. Place the dish in the oven and cook for 15 minutes. Remove the peppers from the oil and drain well before serving.

SERVES 4

Almond Roesti Potatoes with Goat's Cheese

3 large potatoes, peeled and left whole

100 g (3½ oz) flaked almonds

80 g (2½ oz) crumbled goat's cheese

50 g (1½ oz) parmesan, grated

freshly ground white pepper

a pinch of salt

100 ml (3½ fl oz) olive oil

A terrific crunchy potato accompaniment to all kinds of roasts and grills.

Put the potatoes in a large pan of boiling salted water and cook for 5 minutes – they should be just tender. Grate the potatoes into a large mixing bowl and stir through the almonds, goat's cheese and parmesan and season with pepper and a little salt.

Heat the olive oil in a large frying pan. Drop spoonfuls of the potato mixture into the oil (use egg rings to shape them if you have them). Use the back of a spoon to flatten them to a height of around 1.5 cm (²/₃ in). Cook on a medium heat until the bottoms have coloured, then turn and cook the other side. When both sides are a lovely golden brown, turn the heat right down and cook for about 3 more minutes on each side. Remove from the pan and drain briefly on kitchen paper before serving.

SERVES 4

Eggplant and Fetta Stir-fry

2 small eggplant (aubergine), cut into rough chunks

salt

75 ml (2½ fl oz) olive oil

2 purple onions, roughly diced

2 cloves garlic, sliced

1 tablespoon Chermoula (see page 8)

1 teaspoon fresh rosemary needles

a splash of pomegranate molasses

100 g (3½ oz) good quality fetta

Another very simple dish that combines the voluptuous oily richness of eggplant with salty fetta and a touch of chilli heat.

Put the eggplant into a colander and sprinkle lightly with salt. This draws out some of the moisture and reduces the amount of oil they absorb during cooking. Leave for 20 minutes or so, then rinse and pat them dry with kitchen paper.

Heat the oil in a large frying pan and sauté the onions and garlic for a few minutes until they soften. Add the chermoula and stir in well. Push the onion mixture into the middle of the pan and tip the eggplant chunks around the sides. Cook on a medium heat for about 5 minutes, or until the eggplant chunks have cooked to a squishy softness. Turn them from time to time so that they colour evenly. Sprinkle on the rosemary and stir the eggplant and onion mixture together into one mass. Cook for another couple of minutes, then add a splash of pomegranate molasses. Crumble the fetta into the mixture just before serving.

SERVES 4

Malfouf (Stuffed Cabbage Leaves with Mint, Lemon and Tomatoes)

100 g (3¹/2 oz) cooked chickpeas

1 medium-sized cabbage

2 tablespoons olive oil

1 large onion, finely diced

300 g (10 oz) medium-grain rice

3 medium-sized tomatoes, skinned, seeded and diced

60 g (2 oz) currants

¹/2 teaspoon allspice

¹/2 teaspoon ground cinnamon

freshly ground black pepper

2 cloves garlic, crushed with 1 tablespoon sea salt

1 teaspoon dried mint

zest and juice of 1 lemon

1 teaspoon pomegranate molasses (optional)

up to 1 litre (2 pints) stock or water

Cabbage leaves, like vine leaves, are a great favourite around the Middle East and the eastern Mediterranean. These vegetarian rolls are full of citrussy minty flavours in a light tomato braise. They are delicious hot or cold.

Core the cabbage and separate the leaves. (The centre leaves at the heart of the cabbage are too small to stuff, so keep them to make a salad.) Bring a large pot of salted water to the boil, drop the large leaves in, a few at a time, and cook until they soften, which should take less than a minute. Drain in a colander. Cut the very large leaves in half, and slice away the thick central rib. With the smaller leaves, neatly slice out the thicker part of the central rib.

To make the filling, heat the oil in a frying pan and gently sauté the onion until it is soft and translucent, but not coloured. Add the chickpeas and the rice, tomatoes, currants, spices and pepper and stir thoroughly. Taste and season with extra salt and pepper if necessary, then tip everything out into a large mixing bowl.

Lay the cabbage leaves out on a work surface, adjusting them to close up any gaps where the central vein has been cut away. Blob a tablespoon of filling across the base of the leaf. Roll it over once, then fold in the sides and continue to roll up into a nice neat sausage shape. Continue until you have used up all the stuffing. If you have any leftover leaves, use them to line the base of your casserole dish. Place the rolls, seam side down, in the casserole dish.

Mix the garlic paste with the dried mint and blob it over the cabbage rolls. Stir the lemon juice and zest, pomegranate molasses into the stock or water and pour over the cabbage rolls until just covered. Cover the rolls with a plate to keep them under the liquid. Bring to the boil, then lower the heat and simmer gently for 45 minutes. Serve them hot or warm, with plenty of cold yoghurt or Toum (see page 13) or Avgolemono (see page 136).

SERVES 4

Filo Mushroom Tarts

FILLING

50 g (1½ oz) unsalted butter

2 shallots, finely diced

200 g (7 oz) Swiss browns
or field mushrooms,
coarsely chopped

zest of ½ lemon

1 teaspoon ground coriander

2 tablespoons sour cream

salt and pepper

4 small eggs

sumac

sea salt

PASTRY CASES

8 sheets filo pastry

60 g (2 oz) unsalted
butter, melted

One of the very simplest of tarts that requires minimal effort to make – you don't even have to worry about rolling out the pastry! Instead, buy a packet of filo pastry (fresh if possible, so you can freeze any leftover sheets). Then, it is merely a case of wrapping the filo around a ramekin mould to make these pretty and versatile little tart cases that work as a container for all kinds of fillings.

Here we have chosen one of our favourites, a tangy herby mushroom filling, which looks just stunning in its golden wrapping. The eggs are optional, but they do look wonderful, and we just love the way the yolks run, stickily yellow, into the dark denseness of the mushrooms.

To make the filling, melt the butter in a large frying pan and sauté the shallots over a medium heat for a few minutes until they soften and turn translucent. Add the mushrooms, lemon zest and coriander and sauté for a few more minutes until the mushrooms start to release their juices. Raise the heat, add the sour cream and allow it to bubble away until everything reduces down to a thick, sticky mass. Lightly season with salt and pepper, then allow to cool down completely.

Preheat the oven to 200°C (400°F).

To make the pastry cases, lay a sheet of filo out on the work surface and brush lightly with butter. Fold the sheet in half lengthways and brush with a little more butter. Fold and butter twice more, so you end up with a long strip about 5 cm (2 in) wide.

Use a small ramekin (9 cm/3½ in diameter) to mould your tart case. Simply wrap the pastry around the ramekin, leaving an overhang of about 1.5 cm (²/₃ in) at the bottom. Fold the pastry overhang across the bottom of the mould, brushing liberally with butter, to form the tart base. Remove the ramekin mould and there you have your case. Repeat with the rest of the pastry. Place the pastry cases on a lightly oiled baking sheet as you go.

Half-fill the pastry case with the mushroom mixture and carefully crack an egg on top. Sprinkle with a little sumac and salt and bake in the centre of the oven for 10–12 minutes, until the pastry is crisp and golden and the eggs have set. Serve immediately with a salad of bitter greens.

SERVES 4

Mushroom Brochettes with Molten Haloumi

3 large purple onions, quartered

24 button mushrooms, stalks trimmed flat

1 block Cypriot haloumi cheese, about 200 g (7 oz)

olive oil

salt and pepper

Feel free to add any other vegetables you like: peppers, zucchini (courgette) or whatever takes your fancy. The haloumi is resilient enough to be grilled directly over heat. Soak the skewers for 10 minutes before using so they don't catch and burn.

Separate the onions into layers. Trim the pieces to roughly the same size as the mushrooms. Cut the haloumi into 16 even-sized cubes.

To assemble the skewers, first thread on a mushroom, followed by a piece of onion and then a cube of cheese. Repeat the process and finish off with a mushroom – try to keep the mushrooms and onion slices all facing the same way.

Brush the skewers with olive oil and put on the barbecue or grill plate. Season with salt and pepper and cook for 4–5 minutes, turning from time to time – you want everything to be a caramelly golden brown, but not burnt to a crisp.

Serve straight from the barbecue with a tangy sauce like garlicky Toum (see page 13) or hot and herby Tabil (see page 9).

MAKES 8 SKEWERS

Pumpkin and Eggplant Tagine with Whole Green Chillies

SAUCE

100 ml (3½ fl oz) olive oil

2 large onions, finely diced

3 cloves garlic, crushed with
1 teaspoon sea salt

1 heaped tablespoon
coriander seeds

1 heaped tablespoon cumin seeds

1 heaped tablespoon
caraway seeds

1 teaspoon ground allspice

2 teaspoons sweet paprika

1 teaspoon chilli powder

1 teaspoon ginger powder

2 x 400 g (14 oz) tins
chopped tomatoes

6 long green chillies, left whole

1 tablespoon honey

600 ml (20 fl oz) water

VEGETABLES

1 kg (2 lb) pumpkin

salt and pepper

2 small eggplant (aubergine)

2 small zucchini (courgettes)

100 ml (3½ fl oz) olive oil

150 g (5 oz) cooked chickpeas

100 g (3½ oz) pitted black olives

Tagines, which take their name from the lovely conical clay dish in which they are served, can be one of the delights of Moroccan home-cooking. They work best as hearty winter dishes, and meat, poultry or seafood are usually secondary ingredients bulked out with plenty of vegetables, fruit or nuts. In all tagines though, it is the sauce that counts – fragrant with all manner of spices, and often enlivened with a fiery hint of chilli. They are even better made a day ahead of time so the flavours can intensify.

To make the sauce, heat the oil in a frying pan and sauté the onions until soft and translucent. Add the garlic paste and fry for a few minutes more.

Use a mortar and pestle to grind the coriander, cumin and caraway seeds to a fine powder. Sieve to remove the husks, and mix them with the remaining dry spices.

Add all the spices to the pan, stir well and continue to sauté for 2 more minutes. Then add the tomatoes, chillies, honey and water. Bring to the boil, lower the heat and simmer uncovered for 45 minutes. Stir from time to time. It will reduce down to a thick, fragrant sauce.

While the sauce is cooking, preheat the oven to 200°C (400°F). Peel the pumpkin, scrape away the seeds, then cut the flesh into chunks about the size of a whole walnut. Put into a lightly oiled baking dish, lightly season with salt and pepper. Bake for 15 minutes, or until the pumpkin is just tender, but don't allow it to colour. Set aside.

Cut the eggplant in half lengthways, then cut each half into 6 chunks. Cut the zucchini in half lengthways and then into medium-sized chunks. Sprinkle both the eggplant and zucchini with salt and put them into a colander for 20 minutes. This helps reduce the quantity of oil they absorb while frying. When the time is up, rinse the vegetables well and dry them thoroughly on kitchen paper.

Heat about a third of the olive oil in a frying pan and sauté the zucchini until it is coloured evenly all over. Remove from the pan and drain on kitchen paper. Add the rest of the oil to the pan and sauté the eggplant until it, too, is a rich dark brown colour all over.

Add the vegetables, chickpeas and the olives to the sauce and stir in well – you might need to add more water at this stage if the sauce is too thick. Bring the sauce back to the boil and taste for seasoning, adjusting as necessary.

Serve it with couscous or rice and plenty of thick yoghurt. A bowl of Green Harissa (see page 15) is also nice as a condiment on the side.

SERVES 6

desserts

Medjool Date Ice-cream

DATE CONFIT

125 ml (4 fl oz) water

125 g (4 oz) caster
(superfine) sugar

250 g (8 oz) fresh dates, pitted

100 ml (3½ fl oz) Kahlua

ICE-CREAM

8 egg yolks

100 ml (3½ fl oz) water

100 g (3½ oz) glucose

50 g (1½ oz) caster
(superfine) sugar

1 litre (2 pints) thickened cream

A luscious toffee-ish ice-cream, with little bits of chewy date folded through for textural interest.

To make the date confit, put the water and sugar in a saucepan and bring to the boil until the sugar dissolves. Add the dates and Kahlua and stir well. Cover the surface with a circle of greaseproof paper to keep the dates submerged and to stop a skin from forming during cooking. Bring the mixture back to the boil, lower the heat and simmer gently for 10 minutes until the dates are meltingly soft but not mushy. Remove the pan from the heat and allow to cool. When cold, remove the dates from the syrup, which you need to keep until later. Remove the skins, chop the dates roughly and sit them in a sieve to drain off the excess liquid.

To make the ice-cream, whisk the egg yolks in an electric mixer until they are light and fluffy. Put the water, glucose and sugar into a saucepan and bring to the boil, then pour onto the egg yolks, whisking slowly as you go. Add the cream and turn off the beaters. Allow the mixture to cool completely, then pour into an ice-cream machine and churn according to the manufacturer's instructions. At the end of the freezing process, just before it gets too stiff to churn any further, tip in the date confit and allow the paddle to swirl it briefly through the ice-cream. Transfer to the freezer until ready to serve.

SERVES 8

Cherry Vanilla Parfait
with Rosewater Syrup

CHERRY PURÉE

500 g (1 lb) cherries
(stoned weight)

150 g (5 oz) caster
(superfine) sugar

50 ml (1½ fl oz) water

juice of 1 lemon

PARFAIT

10 whole eggs

200 g (7 oz) caster
(superfine) sugar

200 ml (7 fl oz) water

1 vanilla pod, split and scraped

650 ml (22 fl oz) thickened cream

SYRUP

100 g (3½ oz) caster
(superfine) sugar

100 ml (3½ fl oz) water

peel of 1 lemon

1 cinnamon stick

1–2 tablespoons rosewater

1 tablespoon cherry
purée (this page)

100 g (3½ oz) cherries,
pitted and halved

100 g (3½ oz) unsalted
pistachios, shelled
and roughly chopped

A lovely dinner party dessert to make at the start of summer when cherries are in season. Parfaits are good ices to make for those who don't have an ice-cream machine, as they don't require churning.

You will need a 30 cm x 9 cm (12 in x 3½ in) terrine mould, loaf tin or plastic Tupperware container, lined with cling film, for the parfait.

To make the cherry purée, combine all the ingredients in a heavy saucepan. Bring slowly to the boil, stirring gently from time to time to ensure that the sugar dissolves completely. Lower the heat and simmer for about 5 minutes. Remove from the heat and purée in a liquidiser, then strain through a sieve to remove the skins. Allow to cool completely. Reserve 1 tablespoon of the purée for the syrup.

To make the parfait, whisk the eggs in an electric mixer until they are light and fluffy. Put the sugar, water and vanilla pod into a saucepan and bring to the boil. Carefully remove the vanilla pod and then pour the boiling syrup onto the eggs, whisking slowly as you go. Continue whisking until cool, then fold in the cream. Pour the custard into the terrine mould, swirl the cherry purée through and freeze.

To make the syrup, put all the ingredients and the reserved tablespoon of cherry purée into a saucepan. Bring to the boil and then simmer gently for about 3 minutes. Remove from the heat until ready to use. Remove the lemon peel and cinnamon stick just before serving.

To serve, turn the parfait out of the mould and slice into thick tiles. Drizzle with the syrup and sprinkle with a few cherry halves and pistachios.

SERVES 8

Baklava Stuffed with Walnut Ice-cream

BAKLAVA

1 packet filo pastry (usually 20 sheets to a packet)

200 g (7 oz) unsalted butter, melted

SYRUP

200 g (7 oz) caster (superfine) sugar

80 ml (2½ fl oz) honey

2 cinnamon sticks

peel of ½ lemon

125 ml (4 fl oz) water

1 teaspoon rosewater

ICE-CREAM

10 egg yolks

200 ml (7 fl oz) water

180 g (6 oz) caster (superfine) sugar

80 ml (2½ fl oz) honey

1 vanilla pod, split

1 cinnamon stick

1 litre (2 pints) thickened cream

150 g (5 oz) walnuts, roasted, rubbed and coarsely chopped

This is essentially an ice-cream sandwich. The whole thing is merely a matter of baking the pastry, drenching it in syrup and then doing a bit of last-minute assembly. It's simple enough to make, as you can use shop-bought filo. If you can't face the idea of making your own ice-cream, a good-quality bought one will certainly do.

Preheat the oven to 160°C (325°F). Line and butter 3 baking trays, each about 25 cm x 30 cm (10 in x 12 in).

Take 2 of the baking trays and lay the filo sheets onto each one, brushing each sheet liberally with melted butter as you go. You are aiming to have 2 trays, each with 10 layers of filo pastry. With a sharp knife, cut the pastry into lozenge shapes– each should be about 5 cm (2 in) square, and you should get 10 lozenges on each tray. Take care to make them uniform. Spray each sheet with a little water and pop the trays into the centre of the oven. Bake for 30 minutes. The pastry should turn golden brown and puff up a bit.

To make the syrup, put all the ingredients into a saucepan, bring to the boil and then simmer gently for about 3 minutes. Then remove from the heat until ready to use.

Strain the syrup and pour half over each tray of pastry as it comes hot from the oven. Leave the pastry to cool down completely.

To make the ice-cream, whisk the egg yolks in an electric mixer until they are light and fluffy. Put the water, sugar, honey, vanilla pod and cinnamon stick into a saucepan and bring to the boil. Pick out the aromatics and then pour the boiling syrup onto the egg yolks, whisking slowly as you go. Then add the cream, and turn off the beaters.

Allow the mixture to cool completely, then pour into an ice-cream machine and churn. Just before the ice-cream becomes really thick and frozen, tip in the walnuts and allow the machine to stir them in. (If you are using purchased ice-cream, turn it out into a large bowl and allow to soften so that you can stir in the walnuts.)

Now tip the whole mass into the third lined baking tray, smooth the surface, and put into the freezer to set until you are ready to assemble.

To assemble, turn the block of ice-cream out onto a chopping board and peel off the greaseproof paper. Arrange 10 diamonds of pastry across the surface and use a very sharp knife cut the ice-cream to shape. Dip the knife in a jug of boiling water as you go to make the job easier. Then invert each diamond and place another diamond of pastry on top to complete the sandwich. Serve straight away.

SERVES UP TO 10

Mandarin Crème Caramel

CARAMEL

100 g (3½ oz) caster (superfine) sugar

120 ml (4 fl oz) mandarin or orange juice

CUSTARD

zest of 2 mandarins

50 g (1½ oz) sugar and 100 ml (3½ fl oz) water to make a syrup

300 ml (10 fl oz) pure cream

200 ml (7 fl oz) mandarin juice

50 ml (1½ fl oz) brandy

50 ml (1½ fl oz) Cointreau

6 egg yolks

2 whole eggs

100 g (3½ oz) caster (superfine) sugar

Sweet mandarins add a delicious perfumed dimension to satiny smooth, thickly luscious crème caramel.

To make the caramel, first heat the sugar with half the fruit juice until it dissolves. Bring to the boil, lower the heat and simmer until it thickens and darkens to form a caramel. Remove from the heat and add the remaining cold juice. Stir well and allow to cool.

To make the custard, blanch the mandarin zest in boiling water twice, then place it in a saucepan with the sugar syrup, bring to the boil and simmer for 5 minutes. Strain off the syrup and tip the zest into the cream. Put the cream in a saucepan and bring it to the boil. Then remove from the heat and allow to cool and infuse with the mandarin zest for about 20 minutes.

Meanwhile, put the mandarin juice, brandy and Cointreau in a saucepan, bring to the boil and then simmer until reduced by two-thirds to about 100 ml (3½ fl oz).

Preheat the oven to 150°C (300°F).

Return the cream to the heat and bring to the boil. Put the egg yolks, eggs and sugar in a large bowl and whisk well to combine. Pour on the boiling cream and whisk briefly. Now pour on the reduced mandarin juice and mix in well.

Pour a little caramel into each ramekin (100 ml/3½ fl oz capacity), just enough to coat the bottom and reach about 0.5 cm (¼ in) up the sides. Carefully strain the custard through a sieve into the moulds and place in a baking tray. Pour hot (but not boiling) water into the tray to come about halfway up the sides of the moulds. Cover the caramels loosely with a sheet of foil and place in the centre of the oven to bake for 45–60 minutes. The caramels should be soft, glossy and a little wobbly looking when ready. To serve, invert the caramels and serve with softly whipped pure cream.

SERVES 8

Egyptian Filo Pudding

50 ml (1½ fl oz) rosewater

1 tablespoon orange-blossom water

60 g (2 oz) currants

75 g (2½ oz) dried apricots, finely diced

10 sheets filo pastry

100 g (3½ oz) unsalted butter, melted

75 g (2½ oz) flaked almonds

50 g unsalted pistachios, shelled and chopped

50 g (1½ oz) pine nuts

600 ml (20 fl oz) milk

200 ml (7 fl oz) pure cream

120 g (4 oz) caster (superfine) sugar

1 teaspoon ground cinnamon

freshly grated nutmeg

icing (confectioner's) sugar

For us, pudding heaven is this combination of exotic Middle Eastern ingredients and flavours in a creamy, comforting bread-and-butter-style pudding. It looks exquisite and is unbelievably easy to make – what more could you want?

Pour the flower waters over the currants and apricots and leave to soak for an hour.

Preheat the oven to 150°C (300°F).

Brush the filo sheets with melted butter and scrunch each one into a little mound. Put them on a baking sheet, brush with a little more butter and cook for 20 minutes until they turn crisp and golden. Remove from the oven.

Turn the oven up to 220°C (425°F).

Butter the base of a 30 cm x 18 cm (12 in x 7 in) pie dish and crumble in enough of the filo to cover the bottom. Drain off any excess liquid from the soaked fruit. Sprinkle the fruit and nuts over the pastry and then add another layer of pastry. Continue until all the pastry, fruit and nuts have been used up.

Put the milk, cream and sugar into a saucepan and bring to the boil. Pour it over the pastry and sprinkle with cinnamon and nutmeg. Place the dish in the centre of the oven for 10–15 minutes until the pudding puffs up a little, and the pastry turns a glorious golden brown. The tips and edges will be a darker brown, but make sure they don't actually burn. Dust with nutmeg and icing sugar and serve with chilled pouring cream.

SERVES 8

Medjool Date Syllabub with Sesame Glass

DATE CONFIT

125 ml (4 fl oz) water

100 g (3½ oz) caster (superfine) sugar

200 g (7 oz) fresh Medjool dates, pitted

150 ml (5 fl oz) fresh orange juice

juice of 1 lemon

SYLLABUB

peel and juice of 1 lemon

60 ml (2 fl oz) Frangelico or Kahlua

1 tablespoon caster (superfine) sugar

300 ml (10 fl oz) pure cream

SESAME GLASS

200 g (7 oz) caster (superfine) sugar

2 tablespoons sesame seeds

We love the soft, bulky mounds of whipped cream that make up a syllabub. Although they are usually made with white wine or Marsala and lemony or fruity flavours, syllabubs also work well with this rich toffee-ish date confit.

This is another good dinner-party pudding, as you need to make it ahead of time and it needs nothing in the way of last-minute preparation. The sesame glass is very pretty and once it's made, you can stick it in the freezer where it will keep indefinitely.

To make the date confit, put the water and sugar in a saucepan and bring to the boil until the sugar dissolves. Add the dates, orange and lemon juices and stir well. Cover the surface with a circle of greaseproof paper to keep the dates submerged and to stop a skin from forming during cooking. Bring the mixture back to the boil, lower the heat and simmer gently for 15–20 minutes until the dates are meltingly soft. Remove the pan from the heat and allow to cool. When cold, pick out the dates, remove their skins, chop them finely and return them to the syrup.

To make the syllabub, combine the lemon peel and juice, Frangelico or Kahlua and sugar in a bowl, cover with cling film and leave overnight. The following day, remove the peel and pour in the cream. Whip the syllabub until it becomes bulky and forms soft peaks. Carefully swirl the date confit through the syllabub and pour into serving glasses. Refrigerate for about 12 hours.

When you are ready to make the sesame glass, preheat the oven to 150°C (300°F).

Line a baking sheet with silicon or greaseproof paper. Using a sieve, dust the sugar evenly over the paper and put in the oven for 15–20 minutes. You will need to turn the tray every 5 minutes or so, to ensure the sugar melts evenly. After about 15 minutes, the sugar will be just starting to colour very palely around the edges. Sprinkle over the sesame seeds and return to the oven for the remaining time. Take the tray out of the oven and allow it to cool down. Peel away the paper and break the toffee into large shards. Store in an airtight container, layered between greaseproof paper, and freeze.

SERVES 4

Lebanese-style Junket with Candied Orange Peel

CANDIED PEEL

peel of 3 oranges, with the pith

caster (superfine) sugar

JUNKET

3 plain junket tablets

800 ml (26²/₃ fl oz)
full-cream milk

200 ml (7 fl oz) pure cream

1 tablespoon caster
(superfine) sugar

¹/₂ teaspoon vanilla essence

¹/₄ teaspoon rosewater

30 g (1 oz) blanched
and peeled unsalted pistachios

Milk puddings are incredibly popular all around the Middle East, usually thickened with cornflour (cornstarch), rice or semolina, and studded with almond halves. Junket is the very simplest of all milk puddings – all you do is whack in a rennet tablet and let it set. The result is a delicate, thin and faintly perfumed dessert. The addition of cream and a little vanilla essence makes for a richer result, which is certainly a cut above mere invalid food!

To candy the orange peel, place the peel in a saucepan and add enough cold water to cover completely. Bring to the boil for 30 seconds, then tip through a sieve and immediately fill the pan with cold water. Bring to the boil again and repeat this process twice. Weigh the peel and put into a saucepan with the same weight of sugar and of water. Bring to the boil, then turn the heat down to the very lowest possible, cover the surface with a circle of greaseproof paper and cook until it reduces to very thick and clear syrup and the peel becomes translucent. Reserve until ready to use. Before using the peel, remove it from the syrup, drain off any excess and shred finely. Use as a garnish.

To make the junket, dissolve the tablets in a tablespoon of cold water. Gently warm the milk and cream to lukewarm (no hotter than 37°C/100°F), and stir in the sugar, vanilla essence and rosewater until the sugar dissolves.

Remove the pan from the heat, add the junket tablets and stir for a few seconds. Pour into 10 ramekin dishes and let them stand undisturbed at room temperature for around 20 minutes. When firm, move to the refrigerator to chill. Serve garnished with the pistachios and a few shreds of candied orange.

MAKES 10

Chocolate Bread and Butter Pudding with Turkish Delight

150 g (5 oz) best quality dark chocolate

210 ml (7 fl oz) thickened cream

210 ml (7 fl oz) milk

4 tablespoons rum or brandy

110 g (3½ oz) caster (superfine) sugar

75 g (2½ oz) unsalted butter, cubed

a pinch of ground cinnamon

3 large eggs

half a loaf of stale white bread, about 400 g (14 oz), cut into 2 cm (¾ in) cubes

100 g (3½ oz) rose or orange-blossom flavoured Turkish delight, quartered

A stunningly rich and delicious hot pudding, ideal for cold winter nights. This is definitely a deluxe bread and butter pudding – too good for weeknight dinners. It is perfect for dinner parties though, as you make it up to two days ahead of time. The key is to use stale bread that is unsliced and of good quality. Ready-sliced varieties are too moist, which prevents good absorption of the custard.

Break the chocolate into pieces and put in a bowl with the cream, milk, rum or brandy, sugar, butter and cinnamon. Sit the bowl over a pan of simmering water and allow the chocolate and butter to melt completely and the sugar to dissolve. Don't stir, and be patient – this can take a few minutes. Chocolate can be temperamental, so don't be tempted to do this directly over the heat. It is also best not to let the bowl touch the water. When the chocolate and butter have melted and the sugar has dissolved, stir well.

In a separate bowl, whisk the eggs and then pour the chocolate mixture on. Whisk thoroughly.

Lightly butter an 18 cm x 23 cm (7 in x 9 in) ovenproof baking dish. Cover the bottom of the dish with a layer of the chocolate mixture, then tip in the cubed bread. Pour the remaining custard over evenly, and squish gently to ensure that all the pieces of bread are well coated. Cover the dish with cling film and allow to sit for a few hours at room temperature, then refrigerate for at least 24 hours – 48 is even better.

Preheat the oven to 180°C (350°F).

Remove the cling film and carefully dot in the pieces of Turkish delight. Bake on the top shelf for 30–35 minutes. The top should be crunchy, the centre soft and squishy. Allow it to stand for 5 minutes before serving with lightly whipped cream, flavoured, if you like, with a few drops of orange-blossom water.

SERVES 8

Middle Eastern Tiramisu

MASCARPONE MIX

3 eggs

1 tablespoon brandy

1 tablespoon Marsala

100 g (3½ oz) caster (superfine) sugar

600 g (20 oz) mascarpone

MARINADE

350 ml (12 fl oz) very strong espresso coffee

140 ml (5 oz) water

1 tablespoon sherry

1 tablespoon brandy

60 ml (2 fl oz) Marsala

1 tablespoon orange-blossom water

SYRUP

1 tablespoon caster (superfine) sugar

2 tablespoons water

120 g (4 oz) pistachios, shelled and finely chopped

20 sponge fingers

Here the perennial favourite is given a decidedly exotic twist with the addition of orange-blossom water and pistachios – it works wonderfully well.

To make the mascarpone mix, whisk the eggs, brandy, Marsala and sugar in a bowl over simmering water until thick and pale (around 6 minutes). While still warm, gently fold in the mascarpone.

Line a 15 cm x 20 cm (6 in x 8 in) deep dish with greaseproof paper and spread over a third of the mascarpone mixture.

To make the marinade, combine all the ingredients in a shallow dish. Dip the sponge fingers in the marinade one at a time, quickly, and turn over once in the liquid. Then lay them on the mascarpone. Spread over another layer of mascarpone; add a second layer of biscuits; then finish with a final layer of mascarpone. Refrigerate overnight.

To make the syrup, place the sugar and water in a saucepan and bring to the boil, then lower the heat and simmer for 4 minutes. Remove the pan from the heat, add the chopped pistachios and allow to cool completely.

When ready to serve, invert the tiramisu onto a serving plate, peel away the greaseproof paper and pour over the syrup. Cut into portions with a very sharp knife and serve with fresh berries or a cup of strong Turkish coffee.

SERVES 4

Mango Custard Tart with Orange-blossom Water

PASTRY

125 g (4 oz) plain flour

50 g (1½ oz) caster (superfine) sugar

70 g (2 oz) unsalted butter, chilled

1 egg, chilled

1–2 tablespoons cold milk

FILLING

flesh of 2 small mangoes

juice of 1 lemon

5 whole eggs

2 egg yolks

175 g (6 oz) caster (superfine) sugar

400 ml (14 fl oz) pure cream

½ teaspoon orange-blossom water

freshly grated nutmeg

Few things are more delightful than a simple custard tart, shivering and pale, with a dusting of grated nutmeg on top. This version is more bold and brassy – the mangoes make it egg-yolk yellow, rather than primrose-pale – and add a rich caramel sweet tropical fruitiness. Serve garnished with slices of chilled mango for a further touch of the exotic.

Grease a deep 20 cm (8 in) tart ring.

To make the pastry, place the flour, sugar and butter in the bowl of a food processor, and put the whole thing (blade included) into the freezer for 10 minutes. Remove and quickly pulse the ingredients to the texture of fine sand. Add the egg and pulse again in quick bursts. Then add 1 tablespoon of the milk and pulse, adding the second if required. The mix will probably still look like buttery crumbs, but if you squeeze a little in your hand it should come together as a dough. Tip it out of the bowl and shape into a ball. Wrap in cling film and refrigerate for an hour.

After chilling, roll out the pastry fairly thinly on a well-floured work surface, then lift it onto the tart ring and gently press into shape. Trim the edges and return to the refrigerator for another hour.

When ready to blind-bake the tart, preheat the oven to 180°C (350°F). Line the tart with foil, fill with baking beans, place it on a baking sheet and cook for 10 minutes. Then remove the foil and beans and cook the shell for a further 10 minutes, or until the pastry has turned a pale golden colour.

To make the filling, first purée the mango flesh with the lemon juice. Then, whisk the eggs and yolks with the sugar until well combined. Put the cream in a saucepan and heat it to just under boiling point, then pour it over the eggs, whisking well. Now add the mango purée and orange-blossom water, mix until thoroughly combined, then strain through a sieve.

Lower the oven to 150°C (300°F).

Very carefully pour the filling into the tart shell, gently push it back into the oven and bake for 30–40 minutes, or until the filling is just set to a thick consistency.

Allow the tart to cool, then dust with nutmeg. Serve with slices of chilled fresh mangoes and pouring cream.

SERVES 10

Honey Curd Blintzes

FILLING

125 g (4 oz) curd cheese

100 g (3½ oz) cream cheese

2 tablespoons currants, soaked
for 10 minutes in
2 tablespoons sherry

zest of 1 lemon and 1 orange,
finely chopped

1 teaspoon ground cinnamon

1 egg

1 tablespoon mild honey

BLINZTES

2 large eggs

150 ml (5 fl oz) milk

75 ml (2½ fl oz) water

a pinch of salt

125 g (4 oz) plain flour

100 g (3½ oz) unsalted
butter, melted

icing (confectioner's) sugar

ground cinnamon

The tradition of stuffing pancakes – known as *ataif* – is common throughout the Middle East. Typically a yeast batter is used to make thick, fluffy little pancakes, which are cooked on one side, filled with nuts or cheese, then folded and fried. This blintz batter – popularly thought to come from Hungarian Jews – is simpler and makes a thinner pancake. The blintzes can be stuffed and frozen if desired.

To make the filling, in a large bowl, gently mix together the cheeses, currants and any excess sherry, the zests, cinnamon, egg and honey.

To make the blintzes, beat the eggs well, then add the milk, water and salt, beating until well incorporated. Add the flour, a tablespoon at a time, mixing well after each addition. The batter should be the consistency of double cream. Allow to rest for 30 minutes.

Heat a crêpe pan or a small frying pan and rub with a little butter to coat the surface. Ladle in just enough batter to cover the bottom of the pan. Swirl it around quickly and tip any excess back into the bowl. Cook on a medium heat until the pancake starts to curl a little and look dry. You are only cooking one side, so when ready, slide the pancake out onto a plate and cover with a damp cloth. Continue until you have used up the batter, which should be enough to make about 12 pancakes. Allow to cool.

To stuff the blintzes, lay them one at a time, cooked side down, on a work surface, and blob a heaped dessertspoon of the cheese filling onto it. Fold over, then fold in the side edges and continue to roll over to make a rectangular parcel. Continue with the remaining pancakes.

When ready to bake, preheat the oven to 200°C (425°F). Brush the bottom of a large baking dish with melted butter and use the rest to brush the top of the blintzes. Cook for 20–30 minutes until golden and slightly puffy. Remove from the oven and dust with icing (confectioner's) sugar and cinnamon before serving.

SERVES 4

Moroccan Green Apple and Lime Cake

5 Granny Smith apples

90 g (3 oz) unsalted butter, melted

150 g (5 oz) caster (superfine) sugar

zest of 2 limes

1 tablespoon rosewater

We simply cannot enthuse too much about this exquisitely simple apple cake. It is the most refreshing and delicious dessert on a hot summer's day. We first tasted it on a hot afternoon in Morocco at a very swish villa in the Palmerei on the outskirts of Marrakesh, and have been keen to try and reconstruct the dish ever since. Sadly, referral to our journals proved useless, as neither offered more than the most rudimentary of descriptions – along the lines of 'yummy apple cake for pudding'. After much discussion and a little experimentation this is our attempt to re-create that blissful experience – it may not be exactly right, but it works for us!

Preheat the oven to 160°C (325°F).

Peel and core the apples, quarter and slice them as thinly as you can. We used the broad side of an upright grater, but you could equally well use a mandolin or the slicing attachment on your food processor.

Cut a circle of greaseproof paper to fit the base of a well-buttered 21 cm (8 in) cake tin and brush with melted butter. Cover the bottom of the tin with a layer of finely sliced apple. Brush with melted butter, sprinkle with sugar and a little lime zest. Then continue to layer, butter and sprinkle with sugar and zest until the tin is full. Cover with foil.

Half-fill a baking tray with hot water and carefully place the cake tin in the centre. Place in the centre of the oven and cook for 1 hour. At this point you should check the water level, which may have dropped. If so, carefully pour in extra water from a boiled kettle, to bring the level back up to half-full. Cook for a further hour, then remove from the oven and sprinkle the surface of the cake with rosewater.

Cut out another circle of greaseproof paper and lay over the top of the apple cake. Find a flat plate that just fits inside the cake tin, and weight it down with a couple of heavy tins or weights. You will probably find some juice and melted butter spills over – don't worry about this. Leave to cool completely before refrigerating for a minimum of 12 hours, and up to 24 hours.

When you are ready to serve the cake, remove the weights, plate and greaseproof paper. Carefully loosen around the sides with a sharp knife and invert onto a plate. Serve with lightly whipped cream and a dusting of cinnamon and icing sugar.

SERVES 10

Sweet Cinnamon Couscous

150 g (5 oz) currants

500 ml (16 fl oz) warm black tea

2 tablespoons extra virgin
olive oil

200 ml (7 fl oz) water

$\frac{1}{2}$ teaspoon salt

500 g (1 lb) couscous

50 g (1$\frac{1}{2}$ oz) icing
(confectioner's) sugar

1 tablespoon
orange-blossom water

1 tablespoon ground cinnamon

A lovely breakfast dish with myriad possibilities. Here it is at its simplest, but you could add any combination you like of nuts, mixed peel, dried apricots or apple to the basic dish. It keeps for several days in the refrigerator, and can be reheated in the microwave. Serve it warm or at room temperature, with a blob of yoghurt, or Moroccan style, with a jug of buttermilk.

Soak the currants in the warm tea for 2 hours until plump. Drain and set aside.

Sprinkle the oil, water and salt onto the couscous and rub it between your fingers for a few minutes until all the grains are coated. Then leave it to sit for 20 minutes so the grains start to absorb the moisture and swell. Take a fork and work it through the couscous to break down any lumps.

Tip the couscous into a steamer lined with a tea-towel and seal around the sides with cling film. Steam for 20–30 minutes over a medium heat, uncovered, until the grains soften and become fluffy. Remove from the heat and tip into a large bowl. Gently fork through the grains until they run smoothly.

Add the sugar, orange-blossom water, currants and half the cinnamon and mix thoroughly. Serve warm or at room temperature sprinkled with the remaining cinnamon and a little extra icing sugar.

SERVES 4

cakes & cookies

Chocolate Pistachio Cake

CAKE

150 g (5 oz) dark chocolate

150 g (5 oz) caster
(superfine) sugar

150 g (5 oz) unsalted
pistachios, shelled

150 g (5 oz) soft unsalted butter

6 large eggs, separated

a pinch of salt

ICING

150 g (5 oz) dark chocolate

150 ml (5 fl oz) pure cream

a splash of orange-blossom water

2–4 tablespoons unsalted
pistachios, peeled, blanched and
lightly roasted in a little oil

A sophisticated and exotic variation on the more familiar chocolate-almond cake. Pistachios are rather pricier than almonds (especially if you use top-notch Iranian ones), but they are worth it for the subtle, yet distinctive, flavour they add.

Although chocolate is not a traditional ingredient in the Middle East, it is universally popular. The splash of orange-blossom water in the icing further enhances its exotic image. This cake is also delicious served un-iced with a bowl of raspberries on the side, as a dinner-party dessert.

Preheat the oven to 190°C (375°F). Line and butter a 23 cm (9 in) springform tin.

To make the cake, melt the chocolate. In a food processor blitz 50 g (1½ oz) of the sugar with the pistachios until they turn into a fine dust. Add the butter and an additional 50 g (1½ oz) of the sugar, and process until smooth. Add the egg yolks, one at a time, mixing well after each addition. When all the eggs have been added, and with the motor running, slowly pour in the melted chocolate.

In a spotlessly clean bowl, whisk the egg whites with the salt. As peaks start to form, slowly add the remaining 50 g (1½ oz) sugar until you have a glossy and firm mound. Add a large spoonful to the batter and pulse in a few times to slacken the mixture. Then carefully fold the remaining batter into the egg whites.

Pour the batter into the tin and bake for 20 minutes, then turn the oven down to 180°C (350°F) and cook for a further 20–30 minutes, or until cooked. The cake will be ready when it starts to come away from the sides of the tin. Allow to cool in the tin before carefully turning out. The cake should be completely cold before icing.

To make the icing, break the chocolate into pieces and place in a heavy pan with the cream and heat gently, whisking from time to time, until the chocolate has completely melted. When the mixture thickens enough to coat the back of a spoon, add the orange-blossom water. Allow it to cool and thicken a bit further before smoothing carefully over the cake with an oiled spatula. Decorate with the pistachios, and serve with a big dollop of crème fraîche.

MAKES 10–12 SLICES

Spice Cake with Bitter Orange Butter

CAKE

250 g (8 oz) honey

125 g (4 oz) plain flour

125 g (4 oz) self-raising flour

125 ml (4 fl oz) milk

3 eggs

50 g (1½ oz) caster (superfine) sugar

1 teaspoon ground cinnamon

a pinch of grated nutmeg

a pinch of aniseed

30 g (1 oz) candied orange and lemon peel, finely chopped

½ teaspoon vanilla extract

BITTER ORANGE BUTTER

125 g (4 oz) softened, unsalted butter

50 g (1½ oz) bitter orange marmalade

splash of orange-blossom water (optional)

There is something rather austere and old-fashioned about the name 'spice cake', although, for us, it sings of the Orient with its honey, spices and strong citrus element. The texture of this cake is rather firm and dense and keeps well in an airtight container. It is fabulous on its own with a strong cup of smoky Lapsang Souchong tea, or if you really want to feel you're in the souks, try it with a cup of strong sweet mint tea. If you want to be a bit more fancy, it's also delicious spread with the bitter orange butter.

Preheat the oven to 160°C (325°F). Line and butter a 24 cm (9 in) loaf tin.

To make the cake, place the honey in a saucepan over a low heat until runny. Remove from the heat and allow to cool. Sift the two flours together and place in mixing bowl. Pour on the melted honey, then the milk, eggs and sugar, whisking to a smooth, creamy paste. Finally, add the cinnamon, nutmeg, aniseed, candied peel and vanilla essence.

Pour into the cake tin, place on a baking sheet and cook in the centre of the oven for 30 minutes. Lower the heat to 150°C (300°F) and cook for a further 25–30 minutes. Remove from the oven and allow to cool in the tin for 15 minutes before turning out onto a wire rack. Peel off the paper when cold and serve with the bitter orange butter.

To make the bitter orange butter, place the butter in a food mixer and whisk until light and fluffy. Stir in the marmalade and orange-blossom water and mix until well combined. Spoon into a little ramekin dish and use as required.

MAKES 10–12 SLICES

Orange Cardamom Sour Cream Cake

CAKE

130 g (4¹/₃ oz) soft unsalted butter

200 g (7 oz) caster (superfine) sugar

grated zest of 1 orange and 1 lemon

¹/₂ teaspoon vanilla extract

2 large eggs

225 g (7¹/₂ oz) plain flour

1 teaspoon cardamom seeds, finely ground and sieved

1¹/₂ teaspoons baking powder

¹/₂ teaspoon salt

200 ml (7 fl oz) sour cream

SYRUP

juice of 1 orange

juice of ¹/₂ lemon

3 tablespoons Cointreau

3 tablespoons caster (superfine) sugar

6 cardamom pods, cracked

1 cinnamon stick

We love the intense orangeness of this lovely moist cake, accentuated by the warm syrup that is spooned over the cake as it cools. The crumb is delectably soft, and the touch of cardamom in the batter adds an exotic note.

Preheat the oven to 170°C (325°F). Butter and line a 23 cm (9 in) springform cake tin.

To make the cake, cream the butter and sugar together until pale, then add the citrus zests and vanilla extract. Beat in the eggs, one at a time. Sift the flour with the cardamom, baking powder and salt. Add the flour mixture to the batter, alternating with the sour cream, mixing well on low speed after each addition. Tip the mixture into the prepared tin and bake for 50–60 minutes, or until the cake is springy to the touch and a skewer inserted in the middle comes out clean.

While the cake is cooking, make the syrup. Combine all the ingredients in a small saucepan and heat gently so that the sugar dissolves and then simmer for 2–3 minutes. Strain and discard the cardamom and cinnamon.

As soon as the cake is out of the oven, pierce the top all over with the skewer and pour over the syrup. Try to ensure it is soaked up evenly. Place the tin on a wire rack and leave it to cool completely before releasing from the tin.

MAKES 10–12 SLICES

Hot Lemon Fritters with Cinnamon Sugar

FRITTERS

250 ml (8 oz) milk

70 g (2½ oz) unsalted butter

1 tablespoon extra virgin olive oil

125 g (4 oz) plain flour, sifted

finely grated zest of 2 lemons

3 eggs

1 tablespoon honey

1 teaspoon orange-blossom water

CINNAMON SUGAR

1 teaspoon ground cinnamon

150 g (5 oz) caster (superfine) sugar

750 ml (24 fl oz) vegetable oil

These Spanish-inspired fritters are delicious on their own, or drizzled with maple syrup, or topped with a blob of whipped cream. They make a fine dessert, or you could try them instead of pancakes for a lazy weekend brunch.

To make the fritters, put the milk, butter and olive oil into a saucepan and heat gently until the butter has completely melted. As soon as the liquid froths up, quickly tip in the flour and lemon zest, and beat well with a wooden spoon to incorporate into the liquid. Continue cooking over a low heat for a further 3–4 minutes, beating all the while, until the mixture is glossy and comes away from the sides of the pan in a smooth ball.

Take the pan off the heat and add the eggs, one at a time, while beating the mixture well. Finally, add the honey and orange-blossom water. You will end up with a shiny smooth dough-like batter. Refrigerate the mixture for an hour or so, allowing it to stiffen and thicken. (You can make the batter up to a day ahead of when you want to cook the fritters.)

Heat the oil in a deep saucepan (or deep-fryer) to 180°C (350°F).

To make the cinnamon sugar, combine the ingredients in a shallow dish.

Carefully place teaspoon-sized blobs of the batter into the oil, and cook until golden brown and starting to split – this should only take a couple of minutes.

Remove from the oil and drain on kitchen paper, then roll in the cinnamon sugar mixture. Eat immediately.

SERVES 6

Honey and Cinnamon Cheesecake

There are endless different ways of making cheesecake, but this has to be a winner. It is baked in a water bath, which keeps the cooking gentle, and results in a smooth, creamy filling rather than the more usual mouth-sticking graininess of many cheesecakes. The topping adds a pretty line of colour, and helps tone down the honey sweetness.

BASE

150 g (5 oz) ginger biscuits

75 g (2½ oz) unsalted butter, melted

FILLING

625 g (21 oz) cream cheese

125 g (4 oz) honey

3 large eggs

3 large egg yolks

2 teaspoons vanilla extract

1 tablespoon lemon juice

TOPPING

200 ml (7 fl oz) sour cream

1 tablespoon caster (superfine) sugar

½ tablespoon ground cinnamon

Butter the base of a 23 cm (9 in) springform tin, then line with a circle of greaseproof paper.

To make the base, put the biscuits in a food processor and blitz to fine crumbs. Add the butter and pulse until combined. Tip into the springform tin and press in firmly and evenly. Put into the freezer for 10 minutes to set.

Preheat the oven to 180°C (350°F).

To make the filling, beat the cream cheese until soft and smooth, then gradually pour in the honey. Beat in the eggs and egg yolks one by one, mixing well after each addition. Finally, add the vanilla and lemon juice.

Line the outside of the springform tin with two large sheets of strong foil, then place the tin in a deep baking dish. This is important as it stops water seeping into the cheesecake through the base of the tin during the cooking. Pour the filling into the pastry shell.

Pour enough hot water to reach halfway up the sides of the tin. Place the dish in the centre of the oven and cook for 50 minutes, by which time it should be slightly firm on top, but still a little wobbly beneath the surface.

To make the topping, whisk together the sour cream, sugar and cinnamon and pour carefully over the cheesecake. Return it to the oven and cook for a further 10 minutes.

Remove the tin from the oven and carefully remove the foil case. Place the tin on a wire rack and allow to cool completely. Then refrigerate until ready to eat. It is best at room temperature, so remove from the fridge about 20 minutes ahead of time and unmould it from the tin only at the very last moment. Serve on its own, or with chilled fresh black figs.

MAKES 10–12 SLICES

Chocolate Macaroons

250 g (8 oz) icing
(confectioner's) sugar

125 g (4 oz) ground almonds

25 g (1 oz) cocoa powder

4 large egg whites

25 g (1 oz) caster
(superfine) sugar

The sweet marriage of almonds and sugar can be found all around Europe and the Middle East – we have the Arabs to thank for it. These Spanish macaroons are intensely rich and chocolatey, with a softly chewy centre.

Preheat the oven to 180°C (350°F). Line 2 baking sheets with greaseproof paper.

Sift together the icing sugar, ground almonds and cocoa powder. Whisk the egg whites until fairly stiff and then sprinkle on the caster sugar. Continue whisking until the mixture is very stiff, but not dry, then fold in the dry ingredients.

As quickly as you can, spoon the mixture into a piping bag fitted with a 1 cm ($1/3$ in) plain icing nozzle. (It is important to work quickly and not let the mix sit around in the piping bag and slacken.) Pipe small walnut-sized blobs onto the baking sheets and leave them to stand for about 10 minutes to form a thin skin.

Bake for 10–12 minutes in the centre of the oven. Reduce the heat to 170°C (325°F) after 5 minutes. When ready they should be dry on top, but softish and chewy inside. Remove to a wire rack to cool.

MAKES AROUND 40

Alaju
(Arabic Honey Slice)

50 ml (1½ fl oz) vegetable oil

125 g (4 oz) whole blanched almonds

30 g (1 oz) blanched and peeled unsalted pistachios

250 g (8 oz) honey

coarsely grated zest of ½ lemon and 1 orange

150 g (5 oz) stale white bread, crusts removed

1 teaspoon orange-blossom water

1 teaspoon aniseed seeds, toasted and lightly crushed

2 sheets rice paper, each 24 cm (9½ in) square

A kind of Middle Eastern panforte, this ancient Arabic sweetmeat comes from Spain courtesy of the Moors, and is simplicity itself to make. It is a bit fiddly skinning the blanched pistachios, and not absolutely essential if you can't be bothered. BUT, the resulting little nuggets of brilliant jade green are a joy to behold. Toast them for a few minutes brushed with a little oil in a really hot oven to make them nice and crunchy. Similarly, it is worth shallow-frying the almonds to a golden brown – it makes for a toastier flavour, and a superior crunchy texture. Once the business with the nuts is out of the way, the rest of the recipe is an absolute doddle.

Heat the oil in a frying pan and fry the almonds over a gentle heat until golden brown. Remove and drain on kitchen paper. Repeat with the pistachios.

Put the honey into a saucepan with the citrus zests and slowly bring to a simmer.

Meanwhile, blitz the bread in a food processor to make coarse crumbs. Add the nuts to the hot honey, and then the breadcrumbs. Stir continuously for about 5 minutes. It will look very unpromising to start off, and after a few minutes it will begin to come together in a solid mass, and thicken to a stiff, almost glutinous paste. Keep stirring and turning, which will become increasingly hard work, until the 5 minutes is up. Then remove the pan from the heat and add the orange-blossom water and aniseed, stirring again to incorporate into the mass.

Turn the mixture out onto on sheet of rice paper, and pat it into a round disc about 20 cm (8 in) diameter. Cover with the second piece of rice paper and press down gently to about a finger's width in height. You may find it easier, as we did, to use a small jar, or a rolling pin to roll the paste out to a smooth, even height. Neaten the edges with a sharp knife and allow to cool. Store in an airtight tin and slice off pieces to serve with coffee as a petit four.

MAKES 18–24 PORTIONS

Lime Wafer Biscuits

60 g (2 oz) caster (superfine) sugar

75 g (2½ oz) plain flour

finely grated zest of 1 lime

½ teaspoon finely crushed dried lime (optional)

2 egg whites

75 g (2½ oz) unsalted butter, melted

½ teaspoon orange-blossom water

50 ml (1½ fl oz) milk

The tang of lime works particularly well in these crisp, buttery wafers. They are perfect as an accompaniment to creamy puddings and ices, and, once made, keep for 3 to 4 days in a well-sealed container.

Preheat the oven to 160°C (325°F). Line a baking sheet with greaseproof paper.

Mix together the sugar, flour and lime zests. Add the egg whites and mix to a smooth paste. When you have melted the butter, allow it to cool a little before adding to the batter with the orange-blossom water. It will be fairly loose and sloppy.

Dot small, well-spaced blobs of the batter onto the baking sheet. Wet your finger in the milk and carefully flatten and smear out the batter to circles around 1 mm ($^1/_{10}$ in) thick. Refrigerate the tray for 10 minutes before baking in the centre of the oven for 5 minutes. Lower the temperature to 120°C (250°F) and bake for a further 7 minutes, or until the wafers are golden brown.

Remove from the oven and carefully lift the wafers onto a wire rack. When they are cool, store them in an airtight container.

MAKES 30–35

Raybeh Biscuits

225 g (7½ oz) icing (confectioner's) sugar

250 g (8 oz) ghee, melted

225 g (7½ oz) plain flour, sifted

75 g (2½ oz) self-raising flour, sifted

sufficient quantity of blanched almond halves

These pretty, ivory-hued shortbread biscuits can be found piled high in bakeries all around the Middle East. They have a delicate bone-dry texture, which crumbles to a buttery nothingness in the mouth. They really need to be made with ghee (clarified butter), which is well known to fans of Asian cookery, and is increasingly found in supermarkets today.

Preheat the oven to 145°C (300°F). Line a baking sheet with greaseproof paper.

Add the icing sugar to the ghee, stirring well with a wooden spoon. Add the flours and mix well. Now use your hands to knead the mixture until you have a smooth pliable paste, adding more flour if it feels too wet.

To shape the biscuits, roll a small section of the dough into a fat little snake about the size of your middle finger, then join the ends together to form a round. Press an almond half over the join.

Lay on the baking sheet and cook for around 20 minutes. The biscuits should remain snowy-white, but the almond should turn a light golden brown.

When cool, remove from the tray and store in an airtight tin.

MAKES AROUND 40

cook's notes

COOKING EQUIPMENT AND INGREDIENTS

Middle Eastern cooking is, at heart, home cooking and doesn't require any fancy equipment to prepare. The usual range of pots and pans, baking trays and tart tins, knives, spoons and other utensils which most of us have in our kitchens at home, will do perfectly well for most of the recipes in this book.

There are some pieces of equipment, certainly, which save time and make cooking easier. An electric mixer is invaluable for beating, whisking, whipping and kneading, and all but the purist would use a food processor or blender, rather than the more authentic mortar and pestle, for whizzing up large quantities of spice mixes and herb pastes.

That being said, the two absolutely essential items for the Middle Eastern cook are a mortar and pestle. These are in constant use for crushing garlic, grinding spices and pounding nuts, seeds and herbs (except when we are dealing with large quantities). Not only is there something very satisfying about the action itself (excellent stress therapy), but it fills the kitchen with exotic fragrances in a way which no electronic gizmo can.

Another item that we use extensively is a heavy ridged, cast-iron griddle pan, which allows one to recreate some of the savoury, charred flavours that Middle Easterners would otherwise get from a charcoal grill. We use our griddle pan daily for cooking poultry, meat and all kinds of vegetables; you could, of course, crank up the barbecue, which creates the same effect.

Most of the ingredients used in Middle Eastern cooking are readily available. Some spices and flower waters might be hard to find in your local supermarket, but all are available from delicatessens, speciality stores and Middle Eastern grocers. We do recommend that you buy spices in smallish quantities as they lose their potency if they sit around in the pantry. Similarly, where possible, we suggest that you buy whole seeds, rather than ready-ground spices. The essential oils within spices dissipate very quickly once ground, so it is better to grind them yourself at the last minute.

OTHER THINGS TO BEAR IN MIND FOR THE RECIPES IN THIS BOOK

Butter is unsalted.
Eggs are free-range and weigh 63 g (2 oz).
Chocolate is dark and the best quality you can afford.
Cream is listed as pure (45% butterfat) or thickened (35% butterfat).
Milk is full fat.
Olive oil is listed as extra virgin or pure.
We prefer to use sea salt.
Recipes serve four generously, unless stated otherwise.

MEASUREMENTS

When it comes to measuring, we think it is important not to get bogged down by minutiae. Many of the traditional spice mixes and dishes have their roots in an oral tradition, and recipes (such that they are) are handed down through the generations. Many Middle Eastern cooks prepare their food by feel or taste – adding a pinch of this or a handful of that, rather than careful weighing and measuring, and this is the kind of 'suck it and see' approach to cooking we really like! Remember, too, that there is a degree of parochialism in this kind of cooking: every region and family has its own subtle variations on a basic recipe. Ask ten different Middle Eastern housewives for their recipe for tabbouleh, for instance, and you're likely to get ten different recipes.

We suggest that you use these recipes as templates, particularly when it comes to the spice-mixes, which are the flavour foundation for Middle East food. Try them using the prescribed quantities, and once you get the idea of things, allow yourself to be a bit more laidback, and adjust quantities to your own taste.

WEIGHTS

Ounces	Grams
1	30
2	60
3	90
4	120
5	150
6	180
7	200
8	250
9	270
10	300
11	330
12	360
13	390
14	400
15	450
16 (1 lb)	500

VOLUMES

Fluid Ounces	Millilitres
1	30
2	60
3	75
5 (1/4 pint)	150
10 (1/2 pint)	275
1 pint	570
1 1/4 pints	725
1 1/2 pints	850
1 3/4 pints	1 litre

Cups	Millilitres
1/4	60
1/3	80
1/2	125
1	250

OVEN TEMPERATURES

Gas Mark	°C	°F	Description
1	140	275	very cool
2	150	300	cool
3	170	325	warm
4	180	350	moderate
5	190	375	fairly hot
6	200	400	fairly hot
7	220	425	hot
8	230	450	very hot
9	240	475	extremely hot

index